216-295-2197

# FLAMES TO HEAVEN

*New Psalms for Healing & Praise*

DEBBIE PERLMAN

*RadPublishers*

**Publisher's Cataloging-in-Publication Data**
Perlman, Debbie, 1951–
  Flames to Heaven: New Psalms for Healing & Praise
  by Debbie Perlman
  Includes Introduction by Hyma Levin,
Glossary of Hebrew Words, and Index to Themes.
Portions of this book originally published as
*Psalms For A New Day.*

1. Spirituality.  2. Healing.  3. Prayer– (Jewish).
4. Modern original psalms.  5. Hebrew.  I. Title.

Library of Congress Catalog Card Number: 98-65464
ISBN 0-9644570-5-9

**Original paperback edition.**

  5  4  3  2  1

Manufactured in the United States of America

Published by *RadPublishers*
2849 Birchwood Avenue, Wilmette Illinois  60091
847-256-4206
www.healingpsalm.com
Distributed by Independent Publishers Group
800-888-4741

## ABOUT PSALMS

The Book of Psalms, the 150 psalms of the Hebrew Bible, is recognized as the most famous collection of religious poetry. The psalms are traditionally associated with King David. While his authorship of all of them is unlikely – some psalms reflect events which occurred subsequent to David's life in the tenth century B.C.E. – his connection to psalms remains very strong. David was thought to have encouraged psalm singers during the First Temple period; he is described in the Bible as a player of the lyre; he is identified as the "sweet singer of Israel."

Psalms have become a permanent part of our worship and are written in a wide variety of literary styles. Their length varies. Psalm 117, part of the *Hallel* prayers recited during the Pilgrimage Festivals, is a scant two verses. Psalm 119 is an acrostic which includes 176 verses. The twenty-two letters of the Hebrew alphabet each begin eight verses. During traditional Jewish morning worship a specific psalm is associated with and read for each day of the week. Psalm 23, "The Lord Is My Shepherd; I Shall Not Want," is a standard part of funerals and memorial services.

The Hebrew name for Psalms is *Tehillim*. The root of the word means praise. The psalms are a remarkable collection of poems in praise of God. They are poems which reflect the continuum of the human experience, from one person's relationship with God to the relationship of an entire community with God. They contain thoughts of anguish, praise, doubt, thanksgiving, compassion and longing. The words are powerful and sincere and able to be spoken by all of us. Psalms are a vehicle which has allowed people to express a personal and profound relationship with their God.

As Psalmist-in-Residence at Beth Emet The Free Synagogue, Debbie Perlman has brought psalms into the consciousness of the community. The psalms she writes are read and recited just as King David's have been - to express joy and sorrow, gratitude and reflection. Her psalms set the mood for worship and provide moments for personal meditation. Ms. Perlman has brought King David's psalms to life by bringing us new psalms. She reminds us that through psalms, God speaks to us today as easily as God spoke to our ancestors.

Hyma J. Levin
*Director of Education*
Beth Emet The Free Synagogue
Evanston, Illinois

## FINDING PSALMS

I have a fragmented, but vivid memory of creating
a greeting card with Psalm 121 as its motif. I am
in junior high school, and we have learned to make
linoleum block prints. I can feel the brayer in my
hand and smell the sticky orange block printing
ink as I roll it out on the glass, press on translucent
rice paper. The image is a circle caressed by a
crescent moon. Inside, the message in red felt tip
pen:

> "May the sun not smite you by day,
> nor the moon by night."

Where did *this* come from? I am not sure.

It is fifteen years later. The pale, embarrassed face
of the hospital chaplain swims before me as I sit
weeping with the terror of my news. Making his
rounds, he stands just inside the doorway, but
offers no ancient comfort words . He has no ritual,
no prayer book, no laying on of hands. I have no
words to comfort myself but "God, oh God."

Now my husband Reid and I are preparing for our
daughter's naming ceremony. It has been delayed;
Eve-Gerri is nearly three. I have lived past hospi-
talizations and advanced cancer diagnosis,

struggled through chemotherapy and radiation treatments. Side effects, surgeries, recurrence. I am busy with a growing baby, with the strange tasks of daily living necessitated by my illness. We join the local synagogue. Suddenly Sisterhood women, kind strangers, arrive daily for four weeks of trips to the hospital, the wait for radiation treatment, trips home. I am reading *The Jewish Catalog*, thinking of building a *sukkah*. Something in me is stretching, reaching. Something is missing. Where do I begin?

For the naming ceremony, our rabbi suggests I look at Psalm 119, which has verses for every letter of the *aleph-bet,* the Hebrew alphabet, mixing and matching to create an individualized "Psalm 119 for *Chavah-Gevurah*." I write an anagrammatic poem-prayer for her English name. Grandparents and god-parents read these psalms during the service.

Growing up Jewish in the 60s, I depended on what I picked up at the open-to-all temple youth group, from a bit of reading, and from my family's home observance of Passover and Chanukah. We were not members of a synagogue. My Hebrew was strictly by rote. I was untrained and felt inadequate; I didn't know enough to make the pieces fit together. I was unprepared to harness my faith.

We move to be closer to Reid's work. We send our daughter to religious and Hebrew school; I send myself. E.G. and I were called to the Torah the same year. All the while, through more illness, through the triumph of kicking cigarettes and ending my dependency on pain medications, as I move into disability, coherence and stability, my prayer voice is maturing.

The winter of 1991, we take a trip to Israel. A cold, frustrating trip: more snow has fallen in Jerusalem than in 40 years. I stand outside the shop at *Yad Vashem,* the Holocaust Memorial, and weep. I can go nowhere. The paths are too icy and Reid cannot push my wheelchair through the frozen slush. But I have with me a palm-sized Book of Psalms purchased the day before at the Israel Museum. While Reid and E.G. visit the buildings, I stand and weep reading King David's Psalms by sun falling through bare branches.

I did not set out to write psalms. The first one was written for a dear friend; about to undergo surgery, she was frightened by the surrender of control. I found verses of Psalm 119 to comfort her. And then there was something else to say. My friend was also my teacher. She taught me to read my first Hebrew word, to read and understand *Sh'ma*, to taste the nuance of "Hear and Listen."

A friend from former days phones, a gifted musician, who had *shlepped* my kid with her own to nursery school all the weeks I struggled with radiation treatments and chemotherapy. She calls with her anguishing tale of breast cancer recurrence, weeping: "How did you feel when they

said you might not make it?" Asking for an
answer I did not have. Then I did. It was TWO.

After these first psalms, the words began to be
poured into me. They woke me and sang in my
dreams, sustaining me through a long dark winter,
a never-did-arrive Chicago spring. I discovered
that in some unshakable way, I had been called to
write these words. The ancient rhythms that stirred
King David and the other psalmists were reverber-
ating in me. Somehow, I belonged. I was next in
that line.

My psalms have had remarkable results. I find my
glass brimming, as I meet and speak with people
who pray with my words, who are moved by them.
My psalms release me from the disability that
keeps me hooked to oxygen, bent and with a cane,
walking slowly. They remind me again and again
of my survival, my tenacity, the blessings of good
husband and family and friends.

When I write, I let go of the anger and the fright.
When I hear my words read in communal worship,
I am as transfixed as the first time I read them on
my computer screen. These words strengthen my
faith in my ability to weave a lasting thread in the
pattern of holiness, bound tightly to God's design.

ACKNOWLEDGEMENTS
My path to psalms had many helpers.

Hyma Levin, my friend and teacher; Beth
Liebman, who claims I am "channeling" for King
David; Claire Steckman, *z"l*, whose life music
inspired my own.

Beth Emet's Rabbi Peter Knobel, who honors me
by reading my work from the *bimah*, Cantor Jeff
Klepper, whose creativity inspires my own, Rabbi
Eleanor Smith, who feeds my ego. I am sur-
rounded by an alphabet of dear ones, especially Z.

I am grateful to my mother, Beverly Myrow, who
gave me a sense of rhythm and wonder; my dad,
Gerald Myrow, *z"l*, a music maker who died much
too soon; and my parents-in-law, Estelle and
Stanley Perlman, whose encouragement is continu-
ous.

Reid and E.G. are my sustenance.

May these flames rise to heaven,
moving us all from strength to strength.

Debbie Perlman
Wilmette, Illinois
January 28, 1998
*Rosh Chodesh Shevat*, 5758

# ONE

*A Song for Comfort Before Surgery*
*For H.J.L.*

Listen!

Because I know You will hear me
As I fear this unknown I must enter,
Surrendering my self, my authority,
If only for a brief while.

Listen!

Because I know You will hear
As I praise You at this season
Spreading warmth of renewal over cold earth,
Even as my soul's chill is warmed.

Listen!

Because I know You are there:
Hearing me,
Warming me,
Renewing me,
Leading me through this time
To a place of health and vigor.

## TWO

*A Song for the Time of Treatment*
*For C.R.S., z"l*

And I will praise You with clear sweet tones,
Singing Your gift as I gather my courage,
Hearing the music of my life,
As, once again, I gird myself for battle.

And I will praise You with melodies
Remembered from my girlhood,
Songs that comfort me in night's darkness,
That relieve pain as I call forth their echoes.

And I will praise You with measures counted
In perfect stillness,
As machines whir and focus their healing beams,
As fluids rush through clear tubing.

And I will praise You, seeking harmony
In the discord of this illness,
Seeking to hear again the sounds of strength
Above the cacophony of this invader.

And I will continually praise You,
All the days of my life.

# THREE
*After Returning to Work*
*For E.L.L.*


From the flurry of my life, I will praise You.

As I drive the child-circle errand-round,
Hurrying to meet allotted times,
I will stop for You,
To marvel at Your creation.

From the tasks that await me,
That tempt me to focus on minutia
Of hometasks, and homework, and jobwork,
I will pause for You,
To remember Your goodness.

From my perpetual self-reproof:
Is it enough, could it be better,
One more effort, a different preparation,
I will tarry for You
To praise Your Name.

In this fullness of my life, O God,
Calm my constant motion,
Quiet my pursuit,
That I may wait for You with a serene soul.

## FOUR
*A Song for Combined Choirs*

Together we sing Hallelujah.

With many voices singing, we come before You,
Joined in multilayered harmonies;
Ancient chants and recent chords,
Build a tower of ascending melody.

How can we praise God in one voice?
How can we sing Your song with varied timbre?

Listen, O Eternal, to the chords that grow;
Listen, as Your tone within us is altered
By the songs of our days,
Is varied by the cadence of our lives.

Yet it sounds out,
Pure as You have placed it within our throats,
Glowing as moonlight
Through the atmosphere of the city,
Rising, shaded and changed, to fill the ear
With the melody of the Holy One.

Together we sing Hallelujah.

# FIVE

*A Lullaby for Courage*
*z"l: E.F.L.*

O Eternal, hold me with gentleness
Through this long night of pain;
Lay Your cool hand upon my body.
As a mother strokes the fevered brow
Of her beloved child,
Give me succor.

O Eternal, clasp me to Your bosom,
And rock me with quiet motion,
To and fro as the seconds pass,
Waiting, waiting for the next relief,
Stretching endlessly toward the dawn.

O Eternal, sing me to calm,
Humming a lullaby my grandmother sang
As she arranged the soup bowl on the tray,
And brought it to me with the warmth of her smile.
Sing me that song to soothe my soul.

O Eternal, guard me through this darkness.
Wrap me in a soft, warm quilt of Your regard
That I might find a paragraph of flickering comfort
To read and remember
Within this long, grim novel.

O Eternal, keep me safe through this night;
And let the morning come to renew me,
To turn me, to heal me,
To find me enfolded in the vigor of Your love.

# SIX
*A Song of Community*

Assemble us, O God.
Convene us with the *shofar* call of Your love,
That we might draw near to You
As we draw near to each other.

Bless us, O God,
With Your light,
Shining in the human interactions
That nurture our growth.

Connect us, O God,
As, reaching tentative hands,
One to the next,
We feel Your hand upon our own.

Discover us, O God,
As we search for meaning;
Lift us, trembling, to rise
Renewed before Your presence.

Follow us, O God,
As we move through our days,
Finding Your hand
Each time we open our own.

Gather us, O God,
Enfold this community;
As the Grower gathers sheaves together,
Bind our hearts.

Honor us, O God,
With the affection of our loved ones,
Whose faces smile with Your mouth,
Whose eyes dance with divine mirth.

Join us together, O God,
That, embraced in the arms of Your people,
We shelter in Your house,
Secure in Your regard.

# SEVEN
*A Song for Celebration*

Join the song of the Eternal.
Sing the melody of the One Who created sound,
Who gave timbre to the stars
And tongue to the earth,
Whose chant pulses across the hills
To echo in the hearts of all who long for song.

Join the dance of the Eternal.
Slide feet together, bend and bow,
To honor the One Who created dance,
Who made us to move rhythmically,
To sway with the earth's heartbeat
And skip beneath moonlight,
Limbs and brain in meter.

Join the tale of the Eternal.
Hear the story of the One Who created speech,
Who shaded meanings and uttered rhymes,
Giving us tales to tell by candlelight and
    in darkness,
To thrill and to bind and to teach,
That we might know our own stories.

# EIGHT
*For Courage*

You fly, O Eternal,
Between the heavens and the earth,
Multi-colored plumage
Leaving paths of brilliance
To lead my soul to You.

Circle back, O Flier;
As I turn to follow Your path,
Draw me across the sky.

Your wings flutter,
Hovering here, above my head,
Stalling to wait until I look up,
Lingering to catch my heart,
And lead my soul to You.

Beckon me with Your throaty call
As I spread the wings of my hope,
And lift, singing back Your notes.

Slow for me, hold back Your speed,
For my wings must gather courage
As I strive to follow the spiral
Of Your passage
That leads my soul to You.

Guide me on, O Flier,
Diving through clouds into sunlight,
To rise ever higher.

# NINE

*For Complete Healing*
*z"l: C.R.S.*

Like a pure crystalline tone,
Sounding in the deepest fear of night,
So will You call to me
To leave this land of my distress.

O let me turn to You,
Let me loose the steel bands of my dread
And listen for the ringing
Of Your summons.

How can I leave with so much undone?
How can I move away from this place,
And follow, fearless, into the strength
Of Your concern for me?

I am only Your creation,
Striving to create my own remembrance,
To leave this world with knowledge
Of my passage through it.

So soon You call me to Your harmonies,
To close my manuscript,
To sing unaccompanied
These notes of my life, the final hymns.

Still my terror with clear notes, Righteous One;
Quiet me with a silken melody,
That by accepting Your judgement,
I might turn to sing with You.

# TEN
*For Healing*

Surround me with stillness,
Tiny ripples spreading across the pond,
Touched by one finger of Your hand,
Calmed by the warmth of Your palm.

Croon the wordless melody
That fills my being with peace.

Under the spreading tree of Your affection,
I will sit and meditate
On the goodnesses You have brought,
Counting the happy moments like glistening beads
Strung to adorn my days.

Light the shadowed corners with gentle glow,
To fill my being with peace.

Drape about me the dappled sunlight of
    Your teachings,
Opening my eyes to the search,
Clearing my heart of small distractions
That I might find the answers within myself.

Blow the breeze of compassion upon my brow,
Breathing the sigh of peace.

Let me rest by the water,
Probing gently for the sense of what I see,
Releasing my hurts to restore my spirit,
Feeling You guide me toward a distant shore.

# ELEVEN
*A Song for Strength*

I crept upon the trail of my days,
Barely moving, forward then back
With the indecisions of my doubts,
Until I inched into Your light.

Then, casting no shadows, I stood.
Knowing little but believing,
I readied my soul to move into the Radiance
That would begin my learning.

For I have stood too long in this place,
Balancing first on one foot, then the other,
Fearful of moving away from this familiar gloom
Into Your light.

Set my foot upon the middle of the path.
Obscure the tangle of my life before,
And guide my steps to the clearing ahead,
Lighting the way.

Burn, O Divine Beacon,
Send Your light
Streaming through the woods,
Turning night into day.

## TWELVE

*For Jerusalem*

Builder of Jerusalem,
Reconstructor of the City of *Shalom*,
Where can Your people rest
Amid the fury that strangles the towers?

Stone on stone, and cracks between,
Grasping for the quiet
That echoes peace,
Gasping at the pain of discord.

Where are You in the Old City?
Why have You hidden from the marketplace?
I circle above, climbing the hills,
While below the riots persist.

High above, the colors merge,
The faces curve toward the sun
As it turns the stone to gold
And the stone reflects back its glow.

Turn back, and lift again Your trowel,
Gather the mortar and the stones
To reassemble the City,
And invigorate the people.

Restore again Your City, O Builder,
Renew Your people in its harmony.
Clear the rancor from the alleyways,
And the hatred from the streets.

# THIRTEEN

Come again, Life-Giver,
Blow warm breath upon the grimy snow;
Uncover tentative shoots
Struggling to breach the muck.

Come again, Spring-Renewer;
Raise our eyes to greening branches,
Unfurl tender leaves
Hidden in budding limbs.

Come again in lengthening days;
Give us back our ambition
To sow the fortunes of our people
Beneath the fertile soils of Your teaching.

Come again in sunlight and gentle rains,
Nurturing the roots of Your law
With the ever growing sustenance
Of our faith.

Come again as we turn our faces to You,
As a young plant stretches toward the sun,
As a spotted fawn stretches toward his mother,
As the chick's beak opens to her father.

# FOURTEEN

You turn the spindle to form me
To a fine and glistening thread,
Shining in the dawning light
Of Your compassion for me.

Free me from the knots of pain;
Unsnarl the fears that catch
The slender cords
And smooth them as they wind to You.

Fill Your needle
With the strands of my life,
Many hued, many textured,
As You stitch my days.

Unfolding, the tapestry moves to You.
Unraveling, the petit point of my worries
Obscures the pattern of Your concern,
Conceals the fabric of Your plans.

Shake out this cloth and hang it, unfinished,
To catch freshening breezes;
Then renewed, return it to Your hand
To complete the design.

# FIFTEEN
*For Beginnings*

Soar, O Eternal.  Catch the current
Of praise that rises toward You,
Spiralling upward to honor Your Name,
A fine, scented breeze.

We praise You as we open our eyes
To a spring dawn rising before us,
Replacing chill with growing warmth,
Shooing nightmares with brilliance.

At this morning of the year,
We praise You.

We praise You as we stretch limbs,
Easing night stiffness from our bodies,
Rubbing away sleep and strain,
As we welcome this dawn.

Climb, O Eternal, on these songs
Of Your people,
Ascending, as the lark ascends,
Pouring forth melodies.

At this morning of the day,
We praise You.

Hover, O Eternal, in our hearts.
Sustain us as we move through this day.
Remember us as we sing Your praise.

## SIXTEEN
*For Serenity*

Open me to silence, Sound Creator;
Clear my ears from the background of my life,
Quiet the highway of my emotions
As they growl with gridlocked traffic.

When I calm my soul I can hear You.

Open me to silence, Sweet Singer;
Switch off the electronic noise makers,
The automatic switches I flip unawares,
That flap their clamor into my hours.

When I turn from the din I can hear You.

Open me to silence, Word Revealer;
Turn off the inner dialogues,
Still the divisive monologues,
End the gibberish of my misgivings.

When I stop my words I can hear You.

Open me to silence, Source of Sound;
Open me to hear Your words in my heart;
Open me to hear Your teachings in my soul.

# SEVENTEEN
*In Late Winter, for Growth*

Tiller of my soul,
You coax me to growth
With the gentle planting
Of Your seeds of wonder.

Quietly, resting beneath winter snow,
Waiting for the frozen earth to awaken,
I absorb the nourishment
You have stored for me.

Nurture me with Your teaching;
Feed me with Your laws.

Transplant the seedlings
To the rockier bed of the world,
That they might lean against Your edicts
And grow toward the sun.

Toughen me with challenges;
Strengthen me with Your laws.

Rake the narrow spaces;
Discard the debris of unhappiness,
The weeds of hypocrisy:
Pinch back my fears.

Cultivate my heart to You;
Improve me with Your laws.

Grown to maturity, You harvest me,
Bind me to You,
And shake seeds upon the ground
To assure next year's crop.

Gather me to Your storehouse;
Keep me steadfast in Your laws.

# EIGHTEEN
*Roadmaps*

From the center, Eternal Guide,
You watch our steps
As we move on diverse paths.

The route is ours;
The map is Yours.

Give us eyes to look beyond the next step,
To search for the horizon.

The scene is ours;
The vista is Yours.

Give us ears to identify the passwords,
To filter out the clamor.

The message is ours;
The code is Yours.

Give us hands to part the thicket,
To push aside the undergrowth.

The tree is ours;
The forest is Yours.

Give us feet to hurry past confusion,
To stride along straightways.

For we are the walkers,
And You, our Guiding Light.

We are the explorers,
And You, our Native Land.

We are the travelers,
And You, our Welcome Home.

# NINETEEN
*A Song for the Mishpocheh*
*For E.F.P. and S.M.P.*


Hallelujah!

We praise You
With a small child's hug,
An ecstatic grin
From an ankle-high puddle.

Hallelujah!

We praise You
With growing plants and mowed lawns,
With cleaned garages,
With tied shoelaces.

Hallelujah!

We praise You
With vigilance by bedsides
And patience with tantrums,
With gentle pats in darkness.

Hallelujah!

We praise You
With coins in a *pushke*;
With clothes for those who are homeless;
With packed lunches for hungry wanderers.

Hallelujah!

We praise You
With honesty and trust,
With fairness and forthrightness,
With attention to quality.

Hallelujah!

We praise You
In every hour of each day,
By the many acts of our lives.

With the varied ways You have made us,
We continually praise You.

Hallelujah!

# TWENTY
*Facing Life Changes*
*For S.M.G.*

Help me, O God, to find still moments,
Quiet spaces within to refresh my soul;
Calm my questions, my inner debates,
And let me meditate on Your goodness.

Help me, O God, to nurture my courage,
Recalling moments of strength,
Remembering days of fortitude,
The certainty of Your regard.

Help me, O God, to grasp changed visions,
Filmy curtains to blur my unhappiness
And wrap my tears with radiance,
Your hand upon my face.

Help me, O God, to turn to the light,
Warmed face, fingers outstretched,
Alive, alive in Your sight.

# TWENTY-ONE
*For Centering*
*For Z.B.G.*

Help me to examine my days,
To locate moments of fulfillment
Within the hours of misgivings.

Let me plant bright bulbs
For spring blooming after winter's dark.

Help me to examine my space,
To make a nest of comfort
Among the prickles of danger.

Let me fence out anxiety
With a hedgerow of happiness.

Help me to examine my purpose,
To seek lofty reasons of being
That soar above petty trials.

Let me sow feather grass seed
To wave in summer breezes.

Take up the spade with me, Eternal Life Creator;
Take up the trowel.

Together we will plant
A garden of gladness,
Together in the midst of uncertainty.

# TWENTY-TWO
*For Reassurance*

I shall wait in Your sight:
Prepare me with Your teachings;
Place knowledge as a screen,
A shelter against winds of adversity.

I shall wait in Your sight:
Animate me with Your teachings;
Invigorate my days with purpose,
Enlarge my actions with meaning.

I shall wait in Your sight:
Empower me with Your teachings;
Let my thirst never be quenched,
Let me drink from Your well.

I shall wait in Your sight.
Secure in who I am,
I will push back the webs of worry,
To face my daily challenges.

I shall wait in Your sight.
Secure in Who You are,
I will lean against Your teachings
To guide my daily acts.

# TWENTY-THREE
*A Song for Rising*

You set the morning in motion,
Rolling forward, a constant turning.
I look for You as I wake,
Calling Your Name in my heart.

I reach out for You as I struggle
To rise despite pain,
To face daily trials,
And I feel You there.

Pulse in my soul, Day Giver.
Press away dreams and night chills,
Start me on this new day.

You set the morning in motion,
Offering possibilities, an endless variety.
I listen for You as the day begins,
Creating echoes of Your teaching.

I embrace You as I strive
To face daily challenges,
To accept my limitations,
And I am guided by Your light.

Pulse in my soul, Day Giver.
Replace doubt with certainty,
Move my day toward holiness.

# TWENTY-FOUR
*A Song of Comfort*

Turn me toward the light.
Uncover the choices that flourish
When I relinquish my yesterdays.

Turn me toward the light.
Unveil the hopes that grow
When I face my realities.

Turn me toward today.
Turn me to a vision of possibilities,
That denies apprehensions.

Turn me toward today.
Turn me to this moment of extension,
That opens old constrictions.

Before me You place iridescence
To soften brittle sorrows.
Let me rest on the cushion of Your care,
Comforted by Your regard.

Beside me You heap soft pillows
To ease ancient grief.
Bolster my courage with Your kindness
As You support my head.

Stretch the stiff limbs of my confusion,
And let me rise, renewed,
To turn into Your light.

## TWENTY-FIVE
*For the Chief Musician, with Guitar*

In my moments of invention,
I honor You, Source of Creation,
Who created infinite worlds
That I might grow in this one.

You set the questions before me
And give me ways to find the answers;
You fashion a candle of my soul
And offer me the flaming brand.

I reach out my hand to Your hand,
And in that glowing space before they meet
I grasp the incandescent thread
And pull it toward me to form my answers.

Blazing with radiance, I move the filament
To write with new words,
To sing with Your melodies,
Transformed through my being.

Bless me with Your creative force;
Open me to innovation.
Ignite my soul with praise for You,
Burning sparks of exaltation.

# TWENTY-SIX
*A Song of Strength*

Call me on a quest for You.
Call me away from each day's turbulence,
Stilling the waves of confrontation,
Drying my tears.

For You reveal the breadth of creation,
And offer peace to my soul;
You surround me with beauty,
And let me see my reflection.

Lead me on a search for You.
Lead me on through smoke of confusion,
Wiping away the smudges of weariness,
Clearing the air before me.

For You set a far horizon before me,
And offer hope to my soul;
You lay out the distance,
And move my foot toward the first step.

Sustain me on my journey to You.
Sustain me through dullness of spirit,
Alerting my senses,
Animating my tentative grasping.

For You move the stars in their patterns,
And offer delight to my soul;
You turn my head to Your glory,
And touch me with eternity.

# TWENTY-SEVEN
*A Song for Morning*

Let me slide into the morning, Dawn Bringer,
With a smooth joining.
In the last glimpse of dreams,
Open my heart to a day
Poised to fill with goodness.

Let me move into today, Time Maker,
With a firm footing.
With Your Name upon my mouth,
I translate my praises into action,
Repairing my section of the world.

You recall to me my story;
You let me describe its sequel.
At day's beginning, You comfort me,
Offering a Hand filled with courage
To sustain my work.

Let me glimpse tomorrow, Eternal Planner,
With eager memories.
Breathing deeply to set my heart
To the rhythm of creation,
I continue Your work.

You bring me to my beginnings,
To the beginnings of Your people,
Connecting my days to all other days,
Tying my work to the work of Your hand.

# TWENTY-EIGHT
*For the Caregivers*

Show me how to offer hope.
Open Your hand with the colors of faith
That I might begin to fill in spaces
To strengthen another's life.

Show me how to offer comfort.
Point out Your nesting place,
Feathered against the adversities
That wound those I love.

Show me the direction
When I am lost,
Searching to help
But finding no paths.

Show me tolerance,
When I weary of helping,
And a long dreary day
Stretches toward a restless night.

You place before us life and love;
Show us endurance.
You place before us healing and hope;
Show us persistence.

Reach deep within me, Eternal Strength,
And bring my strength to consciousness.
Pull it around us:
Let it radiate with Your power,
Let it guide our way.

# TWENTY-NINE

*For Strength*

Out of my yearning
I sang to You;
From the soul of my soul
I gathered sighs to form Your Name.

Opening my being to all I am,
Discarding vexation and worry,
I devised a new self,
Free to honor the Eternal.

From the center of my center,
The shapes begin their dance;
From the heart of my heart,
The tones sound their melody.

Only when I free myself
Can I be free to sing Your praises;
Only when I loose the ties of doubt
Can I wander onto Your canvas.

Fortify my song with strong harmony;
Fill my brush with bright paints.
Remove the reservations from my heart,
That I might bow before You.

# THIRTY
*A Hymn of Praise*

Hallelujah!
Give thanks to the Eternal!

Give thanks for the journey,
And for the destination;
Give thanks for the testing,
And for the completion.

Hallelujah!
Give thanks to the Eternal!

Give thanks for the rehearsal,
And for the performance;
Give thanks for the kneading,
And for the good sweet bread.

Set the path before us
As an adventure;
Make our steps sure
With Your kindness.

Hallelujah!
Give thanks to the Eternal!

Give thanks for the washing,
And for the folded clothes;
Give thanks for the sweeping,
And for the cleared stoop.

Hallelujah!
Give thanks to the Eternal!

Give thanks for the research,
And for the publication;
Give thanks for the scales,
And for the sonata.

Set the going as an ending
That we delight in our days;
Set the ending as a goal
That our lives reflect Your glory.

# THIRTY-ONE
*Rosh Chodesh Sivan*
*For the Friday Women*

Hallelujah!
We praise the Eternal!

Shining Light Giver,
You create the sun of morning
And the sweet moon light of evening;
Warming our growth by day,
Reflecting our hearts by night.
You offer a beacon to light our lives.

Hallelujah!
We praise the Eternal!

Pulsing Life Giver,
You create quick actions,
And unhurried moments of contemplation;
You open our eyes to discovery,
And to calming spaces for refining.
You count out rhythms to order our lives.

Hallelujah!
We praise the Eternal!

Soaring Sound Giver,
You create the song and the laughter:
The hum of hearts' silence,
The hand stitched melodies
That defy the terror of loneliness
And open our ears to Your call.

Hallelujah!
We praise the Eternal!

We praise You in our opposites.
We praise You for Your creations.

We praise You in our beings.
We praise You for Your new month.
Hallelujah!

# THIRTY-TWO
*A Song of Endings and Beginnings*

Let us sing of our completions, smooth, round,
Silvered voices to praise Your Name.

Every season holds starts and stops,
Years of trees and spirits and souls,
Days ripe with harmony and turning,
Circled, cycled, to order our lives.

Inside each completion,
We hear Your creation;
Inside our creations,
We resound with Your voice.

Let us mold a new shape for our completions,
Fluid and longing, subtle limbs
That lead us onward to praise Your Name.

Every season casts away its jagged edges,
Rubs away the torn moments
To rejoice in the realignment
Of old ways made straight.

Inside each refitting,
We renew again Your creation,
Pulling it taut against us,
A firm bound shield of Your affection.

Let us sing of our completions.
Your hand hovers, blesses,
Bids us move to new beginnings.
Your hand moves us forward,
Toward unimagined completions.

# THIRTY-THREE
*For Healing*

As the farmer turns his field,
So do You turn my distress,
Plowing under random frights
To present me with smoothed ground.

Let me dig old sorrows away;
Let my tears water new growth.
Let me yield up memories to You,
And transform them to Your work.

As the seamstress matches raw edges,
So do You bind my soul,
Trimming away loose threads,
Discarding the ragged edges of my doubts.

Let me sew straight seams again;
Let my needle be true.
Let me orient my heart to You,
That I might seek You in peace.

Then will the remembrance of yesterday
Release its bond upon my heart;
Old wounds will scar with strength
As I wait for the Eternal.

# THIRTY-FOUR
*A Song of Praise*

Praise the Eternal!
You create mighty cascades,
Filling us with awe of Your strength;
You create a trickle of water,
To nourish a thirsty heart in the desert.

Praise the Eternal!
You dance in shimmered sunlight,
Coaxing the earth in her blossoming;
You vibrate in starlight,
To awaken our imaginings.

Praise the Eternal!
You wind over high mountain paths,
Making our footsteps secure;
Your hand steadies our steps over cracks,
Balancing our daily striving.

Praise the Eternal!
You echo through our shouts of joy,
Singing the harmony of our wonder;
You croon a single note
That comforts our loneliness.

Praise the Eternal!
Multifaceted, All Encompassing,
God of All we know and wish.
We praise You.
We seek You.
We wait for You.

# THIRTY-FIVE
*At Diagnosis*
*For A.I.G.*


Sit beside me, O Eternal:
Comfort my soul.

At the clamoring bell of news revealed,
You listen with me,
Hearing my disbelief,
Absorbing my gasp of fright.

Wait beside me, O Eternal:
Comfort my soul.

Recall to me my cherished memories
To bring me forward through adversity,
To stretch from then to now to beyond,
Beckoning to a future You will guard.

Walk beside me, O Eternal:
Comfort my soul.

Help me find the broken pieces,
Gathering them to my trembling hand,
Raw materials for my future life.
Let me find Your hand in this design.

Watch beside me, O Eternal:
Comfort my soul.

Reform me to a different vessel:
Altered by dark fires of fortune,
Hardened in an unknown kiln,
Burning away the superficial.

Wrap me in Your healing light,
Wrap me in Your healing care.

# THIRTY-SIX

*For the Waiting Ones*
*For J.E.A.*


Rest beside me, Blessed Watcher.
Clasp my hand as I startle awake,
Remembering as dreams fade,
Hearing again the pounding of my heart.

Soothe my brow, Loving Hand,
Smoothing furrows of worry,
Wiping tears that fall unnoticed
As I fumble to awareness.

In an instant, our life is arrayed before me.
Happy moments tumble beneath reality's feet.
I reach for Your hand as mine reaches out,
Hands calming, fears in brief retreat.

Support me as I wait and worry,
Snapping back my anger at these changed plans;
Space our days with pockets of relief,
Strengthening moments to move forward.

Let tomorrow's rising find me stronger.
Pushing the tight bands of fear away;
Gird me rather with the courage of Your attention,
Waiting in the light.

# THIRTY-SEVEN

When I turn away from You, O Eternal,
I turn from myself.
I revolve back and back, never forth,
Stuck in this half circle of unhappiness.

Reach Your hand to me.
Push me away from my despair
With Your steady hand.

Like a branch snagged in rushing waters,
I beat against my fate, tiring my heart,
Wounding my spirit.
Yet I will not be moved.

Reach Your hand to me.
Lift me beyond the sticking place
To shoot through rapids.

Before me looms uncertainty,
Behind me, desperation.
Birth me into the void
With Your strong hand.

There will I reach for You,
And begin the long revolution home.

# THIRTY-EIGHT
*A Song of Praise*

Hallelujah!
You open Your hand
Cascading light upon the earth,
Illuminating our days.

So may our acts prolong Your light.

Hallelujah!
You open Your hand
Spilling radiance upon the night,
Safeguarding darkness.

So may our deeds echo Your nightsong.

Hallelujah!
You open Your hand
And sculpt billowing rain clouds,
Nourishing Your creations.

So may we give succor in Your Name.

We remember Your kindnesses
In every hallelujah;
We recall Your creation
When we create goodness in our lives.

So may we be privileged to sing hallelujah!
Praise the Eternal!
Hallelujah!

# THIRTY-NINE
*For Consolidation*

Twine my life to life, O Eternal,
Plied strength on strength,
To nurture my heart and renew my soul.

Join me in a partnership with You.
Tightly wrap my days in duties for Your sake.

Spin around me the words of Your sages,
The dreams of Your children.
Rub my face with the rough weave of women's
   stories
To strengthen my faint pulse.

Bind me to Your Torah,
Four bright blue corners
Knotted together for Your glory.

You are the warp and the weft;
Braid in this slender thread upon Your loom.
You are the texture and the smooth cloth;
Form me in a running stitch to You.

# FORTY

*A Song of Delight*
*For E.G.S.*


Hallelujah!

Sing praises to God!
You plant bright periwinkle
To bloom beneath sturdy birches,
You sustain lichens upon rocky hills.

Hallelujah!

Sing praises to God!
You open rivulets
To meet flowing rivers;
You add spring showers to great streams.

Hallelujah!

Sing praises to God!
You send the yearling doe
To leap through dappled sunlight,
You animate all things.

Hallelujah!

Sing praises to God!
You guard the fledgling eaglet
   who readies for flight
Under eagles' wings.
You make hearts glad.

Hallelujah!

Sing praises to God!
You enliven the world
To recall Your creation;
You invigorate each day.

You give us youth
To warm days that follow;
You sustain us as we age
That the young might learn our steps.

So may we join, young and old,
To exalt You.

Sing to God!
Sing praises!

# FORTY-ONE
*For Beginnings*

Open my eyes, O Eternal, to change;
Fill me with longing for possibilities.
Let my life before be stepping blocks
To what You want me to become.

Open my eyes, O Eternal, to change;
Let me write beyond my narrow descriptions
To begin a new narrative,
Underlined with Your Name.

Open my heart, O Eternal
To put You ever before me;
Help me discard the insubstantial
And replace it with Your words.

Open my life, O Eternal, to fulfillment.
Where before were shadows
Let Your truths live in my life,
Sustaining my actions.

Turn me back to You, O Eternal,
Back to long befores I cannot remember
That beckon my soul.
Turn me back, O Eternal,
Opening to change.

# FORTY-TWO
*Steadiness*

Balance our days, Beloved Friend,
When we careen without plan
From task to task, from thought to thought,
Seeking right paths.

So many days we do not pause.
Rushing on, we lose our focus,
Forgetting the center of our being
Is contained within Your hand.

Like erratic winds, we swirl about,
Rustling all directions, turning dust to wraiths
Across this dry plain of responsibilities.

Running faster, calm evades us,
And the shattered fragments scatter,
Lost and tumbling along parched ground.

Pull around us, then, Your strong arm.
Halt our frantic motion.
Water this arid ground with living water;
Irrigate our thirsty souls.

Place our actions before us,
A rediscovered path to You;
Balance our days with Your regard,
Fill our tasks with holiness.

# FORTY-THREE
*A Song for Courage*

Reach down for me, O Eternal,
To draw me up beside You;
Coax me away from anger and fear,
Beckoning forward, climbing higher.

Grasp tightly as I grope above,
Bind my heart to You.
Place my hand upon the sturdy branch
That eases the climb to You.

For You are the sure Hand
Beneath my elbow,
Guiding my steps as the
Blind are guided.

You are the Light
Shining through dark branches,
Illuminating the ascent
Through strangling vines.

You are the steady Voice
That recalls me from my confusion
And bids me order my days,
That I might turn to You in wonder.

Recall me, recall me, sing my name
That I might hear Your welcome;
Lift me, turn me, to breathe fresh air
Above the forest canopy.

# FORTY-FOUR

I praise You, Connection-Maker,
For Your creations that touch my days,
The changing variety of lives
That changes the variety of my life.

All hearts sing Your praises
On their journey one toward another.

I praise You, Heart-Binder,
You let me know kindred spirits,
Vines growing toward me
As I grow in my own right.

All souls sing Your praises
As they join one to another.

I praise You, People-Linker,
For the faces who lift in greeting
As my own smiles to theirs,
A kiss across a room.

All loves sing Your praises,
As they shine one to another.

I praise You, Component-Designer,
For You see me in all my connections;
You urge me open to new friends, new loves,
New souls to embrace my own.

You create opportunities to look beyond myself.
You guide me in the holy interchange.

# FORTY-FIVE

*A Song with Bytes and Symbols*
*For J.K.S.*

Across far distances
Voices sing together to praise You;
The echos of their concern
Sing Your Name.

Link us in a strong chain;
Forge each link with Your care.

Your people touch in many ways,
By voice and hand and electron;
Responding they reflect Your glory,
Replying they answer Your call.

Link us in a strong chain;
Each link shaped by our faith.

When we listen, we are Your ear;
When we see, we see with Your eye.
In our caring, You raise our heads;
In our doing, we soar to meet You.

Link us in a strong chain;
Each link unique and shining.

Link us in a strong chain,
That we might be ever joined
In Your honor.

# FIVE SONGS
## FOR THE
# DAYS OF AWE

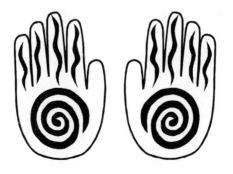

# FORTY-SIX
*A Song of Preparation*

As a mother draws her child beside her,
So will You draw us near to You;
As a father swings his child upon his shoulder,
So are we lifted onto the shoulder of the Eternal.

Succored by the fullness of Your love,
We enter into Your family,
Striving as children strive
To blossom beneath Your smile.

As a grandmother croons an ancient lullaby,
So do You sing the songs of our ancestors;
As the uncle tells of past glories,
So do You recall the victories of Your people.

When we remember our stories,
We continue the chronicle of Your people,
Adding our new life to their tales,
Making new again the ancient miracles.

As the brother shields us from the bully,
So do You humble our enemies;
As a sister shares her treasured secrets,
So do You relay the message of Your care.

Through the daily acts of our lives,
You allow us to praise You,
Making our kindnesses holy,
Binding us together.

# FORTY-SEVEN
*Rosh Hashanah*

Begin the cycle anew!
Turn and grow
Beneath the eye of the Eternal.

You bring us to beginnings,
Yearly, weekly, daily,
That we might be renewed,
Restrengthened, refreshed.

Begin the cycle anew!
Turn and share
The bounty of the Eternal.

You point the path
Away from past errors;
You clear the debris of regret
Away from present progress.

Begin the cycle anew!
Turn and walk,
Hand grasping hand.

Begin the cycle anew!
Start from today, from this moment.
Start from the waking that offers change.
Rise from waking to move forward.

Begin the cycle anew!
Begin from the Center that is constant;
Begin with the Care that never ceases.
Begin.

# FORTY-EIGHT
*A Song of Teshuvah*

You are the Guardian Who protects me
From my self-doubt;
You are the Opening
Before my stubbornness.

You will wait for me;
You will await my turning to You.

You are the Coverlet Who warms
The coldness of my heart,
Wrapping up my distancing
With the radiance of Your care.

You will call to me;
You will call me to You.

For You stand ready to take my hand;
It is I who will not give it forth.
You wait for my smallest motion,
And, reaching toward me, pull me along.

You wait and wait for me,
And I fend off this healing,
Covering my lost chances with excuses,
Uncovering still open wounds.

O let my heart open to the Eternal God!
Let me relax this stiff-necked vigilance
To turn and be healed.
Let me turn and be made whole.

# FORTY-NINE
*After Hearing Avinu Malkeinu*

Pulsing in the life blood of our people,
Pulsing, pulsing with steady beat;
The surviving beat of seasons' turning,
The surviving beat of centuries.

Like the remembered throb
Of our mother's heart
Sounding through the womb,
So is Your love ever with us.

Beneath our conscious thought,
There, the steady beat sustains us,
Grounds us, calls us near
To the Center of our being.

Sounding through our bones,
The bass throbbing of Your rhythm
Plays metronome to our melodic flights,
Stands firm against our dissonances.

How steady is Your love, O Eternal!
The hearts of all Your beloved ones
Feel Your echoing Care resound,
Focusing our lives.

# FIFTY
*For Healing*

You are the Open Door
That beckons me in;
Peeking around the door frame,
I begin to enter into Your glory.

You move me forward, O Eternal,
To step beyond self-made boundaries;
Lift my foot over the threshold
That I might abide with You.

In the house of the Eternal,
I found my questions;
Waiting to be posed,
They filled me with wonder.

Through the doorway of the Eternal
Come jumbled sounds and mingled scents;
Warm sunlight falls across my lap:
All this, all this, Your creation.

Sit with me, Eternal Teacher,
Encourage my seeking;
As I fill my hours with Your *mitzvot*,
So shall I be filled.

Then send me through Your door
Stretching up to honor Your Name,
Sharing out this wonder,
Enriching myself in the giving.

# FIFTY-ONE
*A Song of Praise*

Hallelujah!
Praise the Eternal in our lives!

Weave together our daily tasks,
Each act of kindness
A strengthening thread,
Reinforcing God's goodness.

Hallelujah!
Praise the Eternal Who made us all!

Entwine our arms about each other:
Hugs of caring, of comfort, of friendship,
Shoulders touching, hands clasping,
God's embrace in our lives.

Hallelujah!
Praise the Eternal every moment!

Light the morning of our humanity
With dappled and gentle sun,
Glowing with Your teachings,
That our lives might reflect Your greatness.

Hallelujah!
We give You thanks and praise!

# FIFTY-TWO
*A Song for Morning*

Hallelujah!  I will praise You!

At my waking, I will praise You:
As my ears open to familiar sounds,
As my hands touch sleep tossed blankets,
As my eyes see again the shapes of another day.

Hallelujah!  I will praise You!

You ease the efforts of my rising,
Because I know You are with me;
You linger as I set out the day's tasks,
Calling me to serve You in them all.

Hallelujah!  I will praise You!

Even as my life swirls around me,
Even as the world spins on,
So You will linger with me
When I call upon You for comfort.

Hallelujah!  I will praise You!

I will praise You at each beginning,
For You are the beginning;
I will praise You this day,
For You have made it.

Let my acts praise You, O Eternal;
Let my life today praise Your Name.

# FIFTY-THREE
*Rainbow Hallel for Sukkot*

Hallelujah!
Praise the Creator!

Red crisp apples of autumn,
Shiny and stemmed,
Heaped to fill a basket;
God has made them.

Hallelujah!
Praise the Creator!

Orange gourds swinging by crooked necks,
Graceful as swans,
Inedible and inscrutable;
God has made them.

Hallelujah!
Praise the Creator!

Yellow swirl of leaves,
Yellow fragrant *etrog*,
Yellow corn;
God has made them.

Hallelujah!
Praise the Creator!

Green boughs above our head
Hiding and revealing
Blue and cool skies;
God has made them.

Hallelujah!
Praise the Creator!

Indigo twilight wraps around us;
Gathered in this fragile structure,
Purple wine and chewy bread;
God has made them.

Colored paper chains,
Rainbows of color,
The promise of Covenant;
God has made us all.

Hallelujah!

# FIFTY-FOUR
*For My Daughter*

In this central core of me,
You mark my potentials;
You ignite the spark of eternity
You have placed within me.

I sometimes forget, Eternal God,
The me that lies buried beneath
The faces I must wear,
The duties I take for my own.

Uncover the center of me, O God;
Polish it and smooth it
Like old cherished silver
Handed down from mother to daughter.

I sometimes forget, Spark Maker
That I glow with Your light,
That I burn with passions
That sometimes frighten me to reveal.

Send fuel to these sparks,
That I might light a way to righteousness;
Let a steady wind fan these flames
That serve You in faithfulness.

Then will my mouth praise You
From the center of my being;
Then will I strip away artifice
To praise the Living God.

## FIFTY-FIVE
*Rosh Chodesh: A Song for New Moon*

O Firmament Creator!
You turn the moon away,
You darken the sky above
To let us look within.

In the measured cycle of days,
You give us time for wonder
And time for guidance.
You turn on all the shining stars.

You pull us forward
With the passing days
Until we cast shadows
Upon the night dark pavement.

Then slowly, diminishing the light,
You call us to look within,
To see reflections of Your glory
On the lens of memory.

In the dark of the moon,
We see with remembered light;
In the dark of the moon
We create possibilities, we dare.

O Firmament Creator!
When we expose the light in our hearts;
It can shine in the dark of new moon,
To light our path to You.

# FIFTY-SIX
*A Song for Simchat Torah*

Held against the heart,
Like a cherished infant,
Close, close, enfolded in arms,
Begin the Torah dance.

Rejoice Israel at this day!

Rejoice with voices singing,
Recalling ancient melodies,
Repeating back the *chazan's* chant.

The soft nap of sacred velvet
Rests against cheeks,
Like the downy head of a young one,
Cradled in loving arms.

Rejoice Israel at this day!

Rejoice with crackling paper flags
And clapping hands and marching feet,
Seven times around, dancing, dancing.

Bow with the scroll,
Bend toward reaching fringes,
Lean toward outstretched fingers,
Touch this miracle.

Rejoice Israel at this day!

Rejoice with babies held high
To watch the passing of the scrolls,
To laugh in wonder at the shining *yad*.

Rejoice Israel at this day!

Rejoice in the ending that begins,
Never-ending Tree of our life;
Rejoice in the heart of Torah!

# FIFTY-SEVEN
*Rosh Chodesh Cheshvan*

O Eternal Timekeeper,
You number our days,
You set out the moments and months,
The years and ages of our lives.

Past the scurry and hunger of *Tishri*
The honeyed nights and prayerful days,
The hymns and gatherings
To celebrate, to contemplate, to turn.

Before us the dark of *Kislev*,
The cold sleep of winter
Illuminated briefly by our gladness,
By the telling of tales.

But here *Cheshvan*,
Empty like world after flood,
*Cheshvan*, after and before,
An empty sack waiting to be filled.

Like the sky of new moon,
*Cheshvan* is time aside,
*Far yontiff, erev yontiff,*
Space to dream, time to sigh.

Empty sky for us to fill with dreams,
To fill with songs of courage
For the time to come,
To fill with songs of praise.

# FIFTY-EIGHT
*A Song for Childbirth*
*For D.C.K.*


I will fasten my heart to the Eternal;
My footsteps will not falter.

In the morning of this new beginning,
You coax me along the gentle slope,
Pausing as I tend my burgeoning flowers,
Soothing my worries.

I will fasten my heart to the Eternal;
My path will be straight.

You swirl around me,
Casting waves of comfort,
Calling me upward, onward,
To move through this day of transformation.

I will fasten my heart to the Eternal;
My climb will be steady.

You hold me as I open my soul,
Straining, singing this melody of life,
Feeling You near as I enter a new realm,
Hearing a lusty cry that echoes my delight.

I will fasten my heart to the Eternal.
I will praise God's Name.

# FIFTY-NINE
*Rosh Chodesh Kislev*

Slowly, You ease the chill upon us,
Sending midday sun to warm us;
Through the shattered glass of yesterday's pain,
You move us ahead into winter's dark.

Balance the dark with Your light, O Eternal;
Balance the cold with the warmth of Your care.

You train us to look at both sides;
You give us a month of duality to contemplate:
Two wives, twin sons, a man with two names,
A nation not knowing its own identity.

Balance our questions with Your clues, O Eternal;
Balance our unnamed fear with Your comforting
    hand.

And in the grip of *Kislev's* deepest cold,
Light so brief we could swallow it in one gulp,
Balance the darkness with shining eyes,
Smoothed windows cleared
To broadcast the growing light,
Pinpoints of Your living flame,
Answers to our winter yearning.

# EIGHT SONGS
# FOR
# CHANUKAH

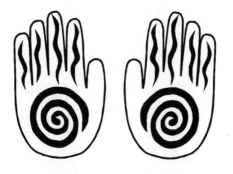

# SIXTY
*A Song for Chanukah*

Your hand holds the miracles.
Outstretched, Fingers curved,
You bring it before our eyes,
Gleaming, infinite, wonders.

Before You, all eyes are lowered,
Hands shielding the radiance of Your might;
Still You hold out the miracles, separating the
   strands
To stream through Your fingers.

Almighty and Marvelous One,
You offer us the chance at wonder,
These shining threads that plait us up
In Your plan for the world.

Almighty and Marvelous One,
You call us to take up the light,
To push aside our spirits' darkness
For Your Name's sake.

At this season, the miracles appeared.
At this season, we must work for miracles.

You open Your hand
Not to pour the light upon our heads,
But to offer it as a beacon
That we might grasp it and move forward.

You open Your hand in this dark season,
As we warm each other and praise Your Name.

# SIXTY-ONE
*First Night*

Brief brave light,
Guarding against the deepest dark;
One finger of Your hand
To guide us through winter's cold.

So long we struggled,
Hidden in stony hills,
Hidden in the valley of our fears,
Afraid of what the light might reveal.

Too long we huddled, hiding,
Pushing away Your hand,
Denying our birth heritage,
Afraid of bringing forth our own light.

Kindle the living light, O Israel!
Light the flame that burns away fear,
That casts out oppressors
And reveals a new way.

Kindle the living light, O Israel!
Light the flame to chase internal chill,
To thaw the frost of denial
And fill us with healing fire.

# SIXTY-TWO
*Second Night*

Paired lights proclaim the miracle,
A straight line defined;
The shortest distance to You, O Eternal,
A clear path, a comet's flight.

So our praises rise to You,
A shining line lifts from paired lights,
Piercing the darkness,
Illuminating dark clouds.

Morning and evening we praise You;
In our going and coming back,
Our awakening and sleeping,
In our search and return, we praise Your Name.

In the duality of our days,
In the right and the left,
The twinned longings and givings,
We remember the lights and praise You.

We follow the straight line to You,
From here to an unknown there,
Believing and following,
Through obstacles, unwavering.

# SIXTY-THREE
*A Counting Hallel for Chanukah*

Praise the One Who makes miracles!

One light in darkness
To vanquish years of strife;
One light is all we need
To illuminate a new beginning.

One is enough, Almighty God
To pierce the darkness.

Two shining in synchrony,
Two lights to recall sun and moon;
God's light in the universe
Becomes our light to use for good.

Two are enough, Almighty God
To reveal You ever near to us.

Three lights pure and clear,
A triad sounding in the darkness,
A major chord louder than sadness
Resonates with ancient voices.

Three are enough, Almighty God
Three nights to sing Your praise.

Four lights define the holy ark,
Cleaned of desecration, polished,
Refreshed in holiness,
Gleaming through the toil of our hands.

Four are enough, Almighty God,
Four corners of Your earth restored.

Five lights trace with fingertip care
The faces of all gathered to work
In the daily sanctification of Your Name,
Simple kindnesses that make us holy.

Five are enough, Almighty God,
To feel Your hand on our shoulders.

Six lights that connect us together,
Generations and cousins, friends and strangers,
Searching together to repair and rebuild,
To banish hunger and cold and doubt.

Six are enough, Almighty God,
To bind our hearts to one another.

Seven lights shimmer like liquid gold
To bless the ordinary and make it holy.
In partnership with You, we choose.
In partnership, we glow with new light.

Seven are enough, Almighty God,
For us to distinguish the path to righteousness.

Eight lights flame, a week and a day,
More than the hand or heart can hold,
But still we grasp it all,
Greedy to draw near to You.

Eight are enough, Almighty God,
To point us toward our future:

To light the path to miracles.

## SIXTY-FOUR
*A Song for Winter*

Strong and Mighty Tree,
Sturdy and ever-growing,
You reach down with nourishing roots
To the very center of the earth.

We praise You, O God;
You stand firm in hostile winds.

Fluttering like winter birds,
We dance among the branches,
Wings half stretched to gather sunlight,
Calling out Your Name.

We praise You, O God;
You shelter us from cold loneliness.

Rattle in the wind, bare branches;
Shake your brittle castanets of winter.
We will trust in the Eternal,
Who guards us from the dark times.

We will fly through frigid air,
Singing our greeting to the Eternal;
We will shelter by the Living Tree
And linger in this holy place.

We will fly, singing praises
To honor the Eternal;
Winter gray surrounds us,
Yet will we praise Your Name.

# SIXTY-FIVE

And Hannah watched,
As one by one the sweet boys perished,
Singing *sh'ma*, singing Your Name
To deny the oppressor.

Let there be no more sons of Hannah.
Let there be no need for death that honors.
Let life instead, sanctify the Living God;
Let loving deeds praise Your Name.

And Hannahs watch as sons are taken.
New oppressors threaten.
Modern scourges, crooked schemes,
Always turning away from God.

Let there be no more sons of Hannah.
Let there be no gunshots in darkness
To slay with random dishonor,
A universe removed from the Living God.

And sons watch as Hannah is buried.
Knotted with the ropes of tears unshed,
They recall boyhood lessons:
*Kibud av v'aym*, and turn back.

Recall us to life, O Living God,
That we might live.
So shall our enemies perish,
And our brave works praise You;
So shall Hannahs' sons sing
The transformation of their deeds.

## SIXTY-SIX
*For E.G.P., with All Manner of Drums*

How quickly are the candles consumed,
Brief, miraculous lights;
Lights only for glory and redemption,
Lights only for Your praise and honor.

In warm arms I held your tiny body,
And lit candles for eight nights;
So long ago, so swift a time ago,
Years' memories are blurred.

Here, even before you could know,
Here in my arms, the candles' glow
Told you the story of the miracle,
The song of the Holy One.

And through the years, as leaning against me,
Your hand in mine, we moved the *shamash*
To kindle for eight brief nights
The shining, miraculous lights.

Now, side by side, we double the lights.
Too brief, too quickly are the candles consumed.
Such a short span are our years,
Too brief a time to honor and praise.

In warm arms I hold you tall against me,
Laughing in the wonder of the miracle
Of who you are,
Praising the Eternal.

# SIXTY-SEVEN
*Rosh Chodesh Tevet*

In winter's cold we are muffled,
Bundled against adversities,
Woolen scarves and puffy coats,
Stiffly armored in arctic winds.

Numbed as well, removed
From temperature's reality,
As the Children were removed
When they sojourned in Egypt.

Is this shielding, this layering away
Of the cold, a muffling of the spirit?
Can an icy finger, creeping through
Awaken us anew to God's call?

How slowly we plod, heads lowered,
Lifting booted feet above snow drifts,
Failing to see the sparkle of Light
Through icy branches.

How much harder we must strive
To answer yes in this frigid time;
To hear Your call to us,
The call to Your embracing warmth.

# SIXTY-EIGHT

*An Anniversary Song*
*For R.J. and A.J.*


Like the horizon's gentle curve,
You arrange our days,
Shaping back, slowly back to home,
Centered on this soul of our being.

You offer chance to roam and return,
To experience and incorporate,
To learn and to tell and to remember.
Still, You lead us, curving out.

Senses readied, we see the majesty
Of Your creation:
Clouds and mountains, falling water,
Forests and oceans and sky.

Senses readied, we hear exotic chants,
And the same made new in changed locales.
Children's voices grown and altered,
Our own love voices quiet in shadow.

You set the taste of each day before us:
A luscious treat, a tangy crunch,
A comfort of soup and bread,
Warm in familiar dishes.

You set before us the love of years,
Of adversity and strength and faith
That hold and heal even as they weep;
You set our loving deeds before us.

You send us gently out to the world,
And gently, return us home,
Filled and strengthened,
Ever praising Your Name.

## SIXTY-NINE
*As Treatment Begins*
*For J.R.*


I stand at this corner of my life,
Looking east and west,
Peering north and south,
Seeking the path we will find together..

For I must walk in some direction;
You call me forward as I hesitate
And glance about me at the passing scene,
Passing hours moving by.

And again You beckon, gently prodding,
To turn this way or that.

I must turn and move forward,
I must turn and choose.

East and west, the path leads Home,
The obstacles vary only in my heart;
South and north, the path leads Home,
Winding back on itself for a block or two.

You will not abandon me as I walk on,
For I trust in Your sound directions;
You will light street lamps
When the darkness looms around me.

You follow me in unfamiliar boulevards,
Noisy paths and lonely ones,
That the strangeness might ease,
And my steps again be secure.

Around the corner and on,
I will walk with the Eternal;
Moving on past trepidation,
Moving forward for Your Name's sake.

# SEVENTY
*Rosh Chodesh Shevat*

Midway through this cold season,
You temper us with Torah's incandescence;
Warming sparks fly as bright arrows,
Your words in our mouths as we study.

We praise You, Story Writer,
As we study and wonder.

You contrast dreary clouds
With bright sun through icicles;
You partner cold with warming tales
Of the miracles wrought in Egypt.

We praise You, Story Writer
As we study and remember.

Warm us with lively discussions,
New *midrashim*, unlikely scenarios;
Thrill us with ancient tales,
Alive once more in our day.

Pull us back in time to stand,
Trembling and expectant at the Sea of Reeds,
And crossing through, to sing
With Miriam and Moses.

We praise You, Story Writer,
Who writes the tale for each generation.

For You will teach us,
And we will be warmed;
We will study and sing
And no longer feel the cold.

# SEVENTY-ONE
*A Song of Intention*

In the worn smooth motions of prayer,
I will come before the Eternal;
For You will even out my ragged breathing,
Comforting my soul.

With confusion of spirit, I search for You;
Yet I cannot find the proper intention,
My mind grows numb as my voice whispers,
Stuttering over ancient words.

As I stumble along, I grow mute,
Forgetting the prayers of childhood,
The psalms learned in maturity,
The ringing hymns.

All around me, seekers pray;
All around me, prayers seek You,
Harmonizing their souls, lost in the whole.
Yet, I stand alone.

Return me to remembered devotions,
Words that have entered my being,
As much a part as my handedness,
My breathing, my eye blink.

Restore me to the songs of my fathers
    and mothers,
The joy and longing of my people
As they sat and wept for Jerusalem,
As they danced in the harvested fields.

Then, with a resolution of chords,
A restoring sigh will calm me,
A sure deep breath will flow in and out;
My words once more will rise to You.

# SEVENTY-TWO
*A Song of Release*

Call us again to gather our children,
Hurrying, hurrying to get in line;
Call us to pack in bundles and baskets,
Only essentials, what we can carry.

Challenge us each day, Eternal One,
To cast off piled high hoards
Of self-absorption;
Let us pack our lives lightly.

Call us as You called in Egypt,
To set out from grief to unknown;
Call us today to abandon unwillingness,
To open hands clenched around fear.

Let us go, let us walk forward,
Away from lost dreams
To a world spun of youthful hope,
A world we can rebuild for Your sake.

Let us find, walking forward, a freedom
Created by our efforts,
A freedom of heart no longer burdened
With meanness and narrowness.

Call us to walk forward toward You,
Freed from the weight of inconsequentials.
Lightened, released, cloaked with Your affection,
We walk on.

# SEVENTY-THREE
*Hallel for Tu B'Shevat*

Upon the winter barren branches,
You paint the leaves of imagination
To welcome *Tu B'Shevat*,
To sing the coming of new trees.

Sing praises to the Eternal,
Who renews life in its cycles,
Sing praises.

Stretching forth our minds,
We see Your winter fields in furrows,
We watch as young saplings take their places,
Row on row to guard the soil.

Sing praises to the Eternal,
Who enriches dust to nourish growing,
Sing praises.

You defend the tillers as they work,
Digging the desert rich and lush and green;
You call those who watch to offer support,
And share in the promise of the Land.

Sing praises to the Eternal,
Who guards the toilers and the givers,
Sing praises.

Sing praises to the Eternal,
Whose Branches shelter over us,
Sing praises.

# SEVENTY-FOUR
*Rosh Chodesh Adar*

Sharp sunlight contradicts icy wind,
Splits into dancing rainbows
As it falls through melting icicles.
So, You bring us *Adar*.

We praise You, Light Giver,
As You temper our days with gladness.

Above grimy snow, a cardinal
Takes wing singing his spring song,
Calling new life, new creations.
So, You bring us *Adar*.

We praise You, Mystery Maker,
When You call us to witness creation.

In the midst of the destroyers,
The heroines and heroes appear
To give courage to Your people.
So, You bring us *Adar*.

We praise You, Eternal Defender,
As our hearts are made strong.

In the shifting days of almost spring,
We bend to changing realities,
We stand lightly, loosely;
You do not let us fall.

Move us into *Adar*, Beloved One;
Move us into changes and mysteries,
Flashes of brilliance to guide us
As we honor and praise You.

# SEVENTY-FIVE
*A Morning Song*

Awake and praise the Eternal!

Awake and throw back the covers
That obscure your potentials,
Smothering quilts of before
That stifle change.

Awake and praise the Eternal!

Awake from uneasy dreams,
Awake from predawn murmuring
Alert to a new day,
Poised with renewed opportunities.

Awake and praise the Eternal!

Awake from dulled senses,
Muffled winter tedium;
Awake to returning warmth
That rouses your dormant soul.

Awake and praise the Eternal!

Awake as a child awakens,
Hands unfolding, grasping for the day
A shout of joy, feet kicking,
Eyes blinking in new born sunlight.

Awake and praise the Eternal!

Awake to this new day, this gift
To share out, more than you can hold.
Awake with a hunger to learn and to do,
To respond, and praise God's Name.

## SEVENTY-SIX
*At the Tomb of the Patriarchs*
*Purim, 5754*


It was clearer in Esther's day, O God:
Your world was smaller, newer, black and white
With few gradations.
Our lives more easily circumscribed, commanded.

It was easier, O God, for *Mordechai*,
To sound the alarm to his sweet cousin,
And point with righteous finger at the *Haman*
Who came to cast our lot for annihilation.

We hang *Haman* upon the gallows he prepared,
And close the scroll to rejoice at our deliverance.
We have moved ahead to ignore the end You wrote:
Hundreds of enemies slain with abandon.

Until, with innocent deaths, You remind us.
And in Your holy place, a desecration of this day
Shows us we must comprehend
The grays of this modern world.

On this day of our rejoicing, O Loving God,
Point the way to peace for all Your people.
On this day of remembering our deliverance,
Deliver us all from hatred.

## SEVENTY-SEVEN
*A Song of Yearning*

In that ancient day,
As *Adar* moved toward *Nisan*,
Moses and the people readied themselves
To move toward liberation.

We look today for liberation
From the anger and hatred that indenture
 our spirit.
Call us, O God, to depart
From enslavement and move toward freedom.

As they sorted their few belongings
And waited for word to depart,
You gave signs and wonders
To confirm Your presence.

Show us today, O God, as we wait
With renewed hope for a modern freeing.
Show us with handshakes among enemies,
With courage to stand against fanatics.

Call us, O God, to dress old wounds
With new faith and new possibilities
As we move toward peace.

All Your children wait for freedom,
O Eternal Source of Freedom.
All Your children wait for peace,
O Giver of Peace.

# FIVE
# PASSOVER
# SONGS

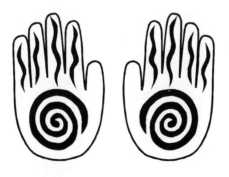

# SEVENTY-EIGHT
*A Song for Renewal*

As *Purim* turns into *Pesach*,
You bid us begin, Eternal One;
You coax us to peel away winter layers
That have kept us muffled from You.

In the gray and lengthening days of early spring,
Call us to turn to You.

As *Purim* turns into *Pesach*,
We fling open windows and fill our souls
With fresher air and warming winds.
Move us to a new beginning.

Call us to You in the changeable, fragile days
That we might be refreshed.

You give us this constant gift of renewal,
Even as You create the world anew each week.
We open our coats and inhale deeply,
As we move toward our season of freedom.

As *Purim* turns into *Pesach*,
We warm ourselves again beneath Your hand,
Cleansing our hearts of debris and denial,
Turning in joy to the Eternal God.

# SEVENTY-NINE
*Rosh Chodesh Nisan*

In the new moon of *Nisan*,
You hang redemption's promise
On budding spring branches
And we begin to ready ourselves.

In the spring month, the month of beginnings,
We thank You, our Redeemer, for the promise.

As a bird calls in the predawn hour,
So You summon us to awaken, to arise,
To awaken and prepare our hearts
For the time of our release from bondage.

In the days of spring beginnings,
We praise You, our Redeemer, for the mustering
  call.

Early, early, we will shake out our garments,
Shaking out crumbs of distress
That itch against our skin,
That abrade our souls.

*Nisan* begins.
We will hasten to prepare,
To open our souls to wonder,
To ready our hearts for freedom.

# EIGHTY
## *For Readiness*

In this final week before our redemption,
You bring signs and wonders:
One Finger, one Hand, two Hands of the Eternal
To untie us from the firmly knotted harness.

In that final week of fearful preparations,
When You showed Pharaoh Your power,
How could we comprehend terrors that appeared,
Surrounding us as well?

Numbed by our burdens, we looked for You
As we packed our simple possessions;
Numbed today by new terrors, we muffle our lives
With comforts, pushing You away.

And our hearts are hard as Pharaoh's,
As obeying current slaves,
We prepare our homes and neglect our souls;
We sweep the shelves clean, but look aside.

In this week of preparation, Eternal One,
Point us toward the burdens You call us to accept,
Taking them up willingly
Beginning to create a new place of wonder.

Prepare us, Eternal One, for the walk to freedom;
Prepare us to cut the binding of our fears,
To find the calm within the terror,
And hold it in our palm.

# EIGHTY-ONE
*B'Dikat Chametz*

From the frown of hurried preparations,
Turn our eyes to greening branches.
You coax from dried stock.
Let us see again Your creation.

Again and again, You hold out spring;
Again and again, You offer endless chances
To be born in wholeness and healing,
To move toward You.

Searching, we find stale opinions,
Molding ideas, burnt crusts of stubbornness.
Peeking into corners, our eyes discover
The crumbled remnants of worry and anger.

Scraping clean the grime of winter,
Built of our worries and deficiencies,
We scour a shining surface, a clean place
To arrange the season's delights.

Sweep us clean, and burn the trite ideas
That stifle us and shield us from You.
Burn away these shattered endings
And start us again on the path toward freedom.

# EIGHTY-TWO
*A Song of Praise for Pesach*

Hallelujah!
Praise the Eternal!

We praise You in the pause before beginning,
The quiet glance and sigh
As we stand poised on the moment,
Filling our eyes with Your offer of freedom.

Hallelujah!
Praise the Eternal!

We praise You as we step forward together,
Hands held, heads raised, eyes focused
On the far distant dream of our redemption,
The place of Your vision for a holy people.

Hallelujah!
Praise the Eternal!

We praise You in the first short passage,
As the children run ahead and back,
Each striving to be the first to see
And call out the beauty of the Promise.

Hallelujah!
Praise the Eternal!

And let us praise You when our legs are weary
And the bundles and burdens are multiplied
By the time they have been on our backs.
Help us to praise You then.

For You, Eternal Deliverer,
Bring us all out of our enslavement.
You open our minds to the freedom
Contained within each of us.

You, Eternal Deliverer,
Call us to adorn our freedom with deeds,
To be released to a dedicated freedom,
Free to praise You with the work of our hearts.

Praise the Eternal!
Hallelujah!

# EIGHTY-THREE
*Yom HaShoah*

We wandered in the dryness,
While our children begged for water,
And death was all around us.
Yet were You there in the desert.

Reveal Your plan, O Eternal,
Let us be Your confidants
That we may soothe our children
With confidence of Your care.

In the barricaded barn, hidden in straw
Our children wept silently
As death rode into the gooseyard.
Yet were You there in the village.

Speak again of the Covenant
That saved Isaac from the knife,
That broke through brambled thorns
As Abraham became Your partner in life.

Even the taste of ashes,
Of smoke and destruction,
Of remembrance that defies forgetting,
Even there, You were with us.

We untangle the Plan from our memories,
And hold it, threadbare and knotted,
Soiled, defiled, yet surviving,
Reborn, released from agony.

You are there, O Eternal.
You are there as we remember.
Your hand beckons us closer.
Your voice whispers: Do not forget.

# EIGHTY-FOUR
*Rosh Chodesh Iyar*

In the long walk of spring,
You take us toward our obligations,
Sudden chill rains reminding us
Of intangible warmth at this season.

Awaken us, O Eternal to burgeoning wisdom,
To tasks we will learn to perform.
Awaken our hearts to sing to You
The melodies that our people are creating.

In the long walk of spring,
Turn our eyes to one another,
Clearing the path ahead, steadying us
As we walk toward matured beginnings.

You have taken us from slavery to new destinies,
Even as You reawaken the earth to growing;
You have started us on a righteous path,
Even as You challenge us with new duties.

Awaken us, O Eternal, to *Iyar*,
The month beyond beginnings,
The month of learning and telling,
The month of new discoveries.

# EIGHTY-FIVE

*In Iyar: Ani Adonai Rofecha*
*A Song of Healing*

After this long night of weakness,
I wake again in the morning of return;
Shaking off the terrors and the dreams,
I open my lips to the Eternal.

You are my Strength and my Hope,
The Author of my healing;
You are my Promise and my Courage
Guiding the steps I take toward healing.

After the winter's darkness and biting cold,
The hidden awayness of my illness,
The isolation, the fear that settled upon me,
I rise with renewed strength to praise You.

You are the Wonder of new life,
Warming, healing sun upon my head;
You restore my concern for others,
As I relinquish my constant self-inventory.

You come to me as spring comes,
Circling back to heal the ravaged earth;
You rest Your hand of blessing on my shoulder
And I sigh with relief at Your concern.

I look for You, Divine Physician,
Even as I begin again to take up my life;
I look for You, Complete Healer,
As I begin again.

# EIGHTY-SIX
*Erev Shabbat*

We cast off the glow of the setting sun,
And hesitate in this moment before darkness
As we empty the pockets of our week's cares
And shake out the wrinkles of our worries.

Beloved Creator, You fashion *Shabbat*
As an elegant garment to draw around us;
We hang aside the moments of our daily life
And close the closet door of routine.

We pause before the darkness swarms
And draw in the sweet aromas of *Shabbat*-to-be.
Then, with a shuddering sigh,
We are as children freed from unhappy dreams.

Beloved Creator, You fashion *Shabbat*
To refresh us, to clear us of our daily turmoil,
To return us to You
As we calm our hearts before You.

We gather the candles' light in our hands
As we praise Your Name,
Even as our mothers praised You from before,
As murmured words detailed their blessings.

We gather the candles' light in our eyes
As we bless Your Name,
Even as our fathers blessed You from before
And rested smiles upon our faces.

Beloved Creator, You fashion *Shabbat*
And wrap around us the light of Your peace,
Even as we praise You,
Even as we bless Your Name.

# EIGHTY-SEVEN
*Shabbat*

Stars reflect off heaven's hem
As *Shabbat* enters quietly;
Other, over, away all week,
*Shabbat* is the fruit of six days' imaginings.

Hushed and soft, with tender smile,
*Shabbat* greets us as we raise our cups;
*Shabbat* perches upon the rim
And nods as we bless and praise and remember.

Come again to us, Gracious Host,
Fill our hearts with peace;
Come sing with us, Sweet Singer,
We will fill our mouths with praise.

Surround us with *Shabbat's* beauty,
All time in a day;
Surround us with the faces of our dear ones:
Now and then and still to be.

Come again to us, Gracious Host,
Come again as *Shabbat* is seated at our table;
Come sing with us, Sweet Singer,
As *Shabbat* fills our home with peace.

# EIGHTY-EIGHT
*Rosh Chodesh Sivan*

We turn the earth and plant the seeds;
We wait for sun warmth and soaking rains
To nurture our labors and send down roots.
So do we wait for the Eternal.

For You have planted within us
The need for wisdom;
You have planted within us
The need for love.

We fear for late spring freeze;
We fear for lack of rain.
We hover over our fields,
Praying to the Eternal.

You do not stifle our fears,
You call us to face them;
You do not indulge our longings,
But reassure us as we discover.

We tend our growing fields.
We trust in You as we work and worry;
We trust in Your goodness
As we send down our own roots.

Deep, deep, into the heart of the Eternal,
Who calls us to learn and to love;
Deep, deep, into our own hearts,
As we nourish our growing devotion.

# EIGHTY-NINE
*Shavuot*

Upon Sinai, in darkness and in light,
Upon Sinai, the hand of Moses trembles;
Below Sinai the people sing,
A cacophony of song dances in the air.

Upon Sinai, with shadow and with fire,
With coldness and with fierce heat,
The mouth of Moses trembles
As he reads back the dictation.

Upon Sinai, in the still air,
Moses nods once more and struggles to rise
As he has struggled these past months
To feel his legs beneath him on the sand.

The songs of the people dance in the air,
Shimmering melodies of delight
Hover in the desert heat
As Moses guards his steps down the mountain.

And the songs begin to form around him,
A spiral winding of pure tones
That dress Moses in a spectrum of sound,
A glimmering garment of melody.

Until he stands again with the people,
And, holding out his hands,
He embraces them with his own song
Of the Living God.

Then did our songs become songs of praise,
Then could all our varied songs worship You
And give You thanks, O Eternal and Beloved One.

As from Moses' lips we were called,
As from Moses' shoulder the burden was shared,
So do Your people Israel listen and obey.

# NINETY
*A Song of Assents*

Let my life smile yes to the Eternal;
Let my days praise God's name.
Let mouth be filled with songs of delight
Even as I delight in my Creator.

So with a nod and a wink and a grin,
I will dance to Your melody,
Twisting and turning a path of *mitzvot*
To honor and praise my Creator.

Let my life smile yes to the Eternal;
Let my nights find contemplation in God's
name.
Let my heart be soothed with loving thoughts
Even as I free it from sorrow.

As with a clap and a tap and a stomp,
My limbs keep time to Your melody,
Counting the beat of the heavens' gladness
That honors and praises the Creator.

Let my life smile yes to the Eternal,
Let my works praise God's name.
Let me honor You all my nights and my days,
Let my shadows be displaced by Your light.

Let my life smile yes.

# NINETY-ONE
*Rosh Chodesh Tammuz*

*Tammuz* is interlude, reiteration, steady growth:
Setting sprinklers, pulling weeds, nourishment
That signals the start of culmination.
Guide us, Eternal One, as we move in our tasks.

No longer wanderers, we have planted our
    fields,
We have set out our fruit trees.
Now we contemplate Your care for us
As we wait for consolidation of further growth.

The longer days wind in on themselves,
Longer sunlight erases the hurry;
Longer moments to linger: a book, an embrace,
To listen to children's voices calling in twilight.

Hear us in the longer days, Source of Growth,
Calling as our fathers and mothers called,
Calling as we summon our children home from
    play.
Hear us as we call You in truth.

Hear us as we move into this time of increase,
As we gather up sunlight and breezes and rains
To lay aside against the unknowns ahead.
Hear us as we call You in truth.

# NINETY-TWO
*Rosh Chodesh Av*

Fading blossoms give way to green fruits,
As You move us toward hot and growing days,
Ripening us, filling us with longing,
Plump and sturdy fruit attached by fragile stems.

Always, O Eternal One, this full and empty,
Never the *chuppah* without the broken glass,
Never sweet remembrance without the *yahrtzeit*,
Summer growing without fear of drought.

Hot and dry, hot and humid, hot and heavy,
Blankets not fully dried from fever dreams;
Yet You uncover the stars in revolving glory,
You suspend the sun's setting in many hues.

Lush and full, the leaves hide and reveal:
So many shades of green in Your palette
That our eyes cannot gather them,
Until we see the contrast of bare earth.

Remind us and restore us, Eternal our God;
Fill us and empty us of our loves and fears.
Restore our balance and nourish us,
Stretching our souls in the hot air of *Av*.

# NINETY-THREE
*Tisha B'Av*
*In Memoriam: L.K.*

Driven away or drifted away,
We all reflect the Temples' conflagration:
Some with daily melodies to You,
All in the marrow-born tears that spring unbidden.

Driven away and drifted away,
We sing Your songs in our faces and our children,
In the half-remembered sighs of our great-greats,
And in the ongoing definition of our exile.

So many ways to praise You,
So many ways to survive exile,
Until, turning, turning, the City is retaken,
Again the Stones are washed with tears of our joy.

But our roots, into more common stones, are deep;
We sing Your Name in many places.
Drifted by human vagary, driven by human cruelty,
Our whole hearts are divided: Home and home.

Unwillingly and unwittingly, we left Jerusalem:
Turn us back to Your golden city,
Praising from new houses,
In time or in place.

Let our hearts dwell in two time zones,
That Your Name is ever on our lips.

# NINETY-FOUR
*Rosh Chodesh Elul*

Fighting the languor of sultry days,
We begin the turning, back to You;
Moving against the heat of our hearts,
Against the anger inside, we turn.

Call us to begin the examination, Healing God;
Call for us to remove the garment of our deceit,
The fears that bind us away from You,
Chaffing at our tender miseries.

In the month of *Elul*, we begin the unlayering,
Peeling piece by piece the accumulated detritus,
Shaking it free, holding it to the hot light
To scrutinize as the year begins its ending.

In the month of *Elul*, we uncover our secrets,
Examining them with a truthful heart,
Counting the pulse beats of our life,
The selfish pressures we apply and resist.

Call us to the consultation of our souls,
For You are a God of healing and mercy;
Call us to begin without delay,
That *Elul* might draw us near to You.

# NINETY-FIVE
## 12 Elul: Ani l'Dodi v'Dodi Li

Here at *Elul's* center, bright lovers' moon
Casts shadows on our clouds of doubt,
Filling the air with sighs of longing,
Sighs of regretting, sighs of grief.

We fill this half-dark with swarming thoughts,
Itching uncertainties that we must soothe
With a letting go, an arms-opening welcome
To Your presence in our days and nights.

You fill the sky with Your light,
Chasing away the dark terror of our souls
Even as we long for You in *Elul's* center,
Even as we seek You in our hearts' center.

Croon us melodies of confidence, Beloved One,
Tender melodies that pull us back to You;
Let us rest against Your strong love for us,
Finding the Source of our searching.

# NINETY-SIX
*Rosh Hashanah*

At the dark moon of our dreamings,
The dark moon of Your eternity,
You cloak us, Merciful One, in velvet mysteries
As the new year begins.

Merciful One, You darken this sky of beginnings,
You turn the moon face of discovery around
To urge us to look inside for answers,
To find souls' light within our beings.

Overcast skies, clouds laden with doubt,
Filled with the tears You shed
For our sake, that our burdens might lighten,
Might lift from our hearts.

Yet the burdens do not leave us,
As moment by year we continue,
Never drying Your tears on the cloth of deeds,
Wringing them out to water dry ground.

Merciful One, in the dark of First Moon
You begin our lives again,
As we give up our tasks for Your sake,
As our souls fly to You through darkness.

Call us again to You,
Call us turning the moon around to reflect
The grace of our beginning,
Our turning again to You.

# NINETY-SEVEN
*Shabbat Shuvah*

Turning, turning, I search for You.
Sometimes I turn too quickly.
Sometimes I forget to keep my eyes open.
Sometimes I look only outward.

Turning slowly, I see clearly:
Hurts I have caused, anger, sadness.
I see the results of not looking:
Broken sidewalks trip my impenitent steps.

Turning slower still, my days take focus,
Until the paler tones of the positive
Appear through the harsh glaring hues
Of the tasks undone, the cruel replies.

Until my revolution stops, and sighing,
I once again see the far distance of the Eternal.
You ask me to try, but do not forsake me in failure.
You forgive me as I struggle to forgive myself.

Turn me again to You, Merciful One;
Turn me again to my own exoneration.
Turn me to these tasks of mending and healing,
Inwardly, outwardly, that I might stand before You.

# NINETY-EIGHT

*After the Accident*
*For Daniel, David's Son*

You see me in this den with lions,
And I cry out to You:
Why and why, O Eternal?
Where can I hide from this terrible night?

For the darkness pulls at me,
And the sharp teeth of memory surround me.
The lions move in fury to attack me,
Repeating the horror and the pain.

You see me in this den with lions,
And I listen for You, O Eternal.
I release the sobs that rise,
And faintly I hear You.

For You will begin to illuminate kinder days,
You will give me mourning and healing.
You will soothe night terror with returning dawn,
To soften memories' teeth with my mother's smile.

# NINETY-NINE
*Yom Kippur*

In the growing light of *Tishri*,
The Gate stands ajar, swaying gently
To the rhythm of our supplications,
Held open by Your love for us.

You call us to stand before You;
You call us again and again,
Not just in *Tishri*, not just in *Nisan*,
But every moment to stand and remember.

You call us to stand before You:
You support us as we sway;
Your strong hand supports our weakness,
Born of this life's hungers.

You call us to gather and stand,
Crying out our longing and our fears:
We can choose but You must decide
What loves and terrors will surround us.

You call us to stand and to gather,
Joining the energies of our hands
To the life choice You offer us,
Choosing life that we might give.

You call us, young and old, to the Gate.
You call us to heed Your words before us
And transform them to our modern tasks:
Praising, praising the Eternal God.

# ONE HUNDRED
*A Song of Healing and Praise*

Sing praises to the Eternal!
Sing songs for a new day!

You draw around me the warmth of sleep;
Yet I am stirred to restlessness by my songs.
Dreaming, longing, I rouse and sing to You.
In the murmuring hours of darkness, I praise You.

You awaken me to morning brilliance;
Moving with pain I rise to greet You.
Yet You continuously restore me
As I push forward and greet this day.

I will praise You, O Eternal,
Not in my infirmities, but in my life;
You do not harm me in anger,
But preserve me with challenges.

I will sing new songs as I gather my strength;
I will sing Your praise as I gasp in wonder
At this sweetness of light, the kind hands
That are Your hand to ease my days.

I will sing You the song that dampens my eyes,
The song of tears and pain and rage
That releases to You and then is healed
As I learn my adaptations of living.

I will sing You praises with perfect surety,
For I trust in You with all my heart.
I will sing You a song for a new day,
A song to the Eternal God.

# ONE HUNDRED ONE
*Rosh Chodesh Cheshvan*

And suddenly, *Cheshvan* is here
In the cooling, darkening days;
While the *etrog*'s fragrance lingers,
You turn aside the moon.

The thrilling, awesome cycle revolves again,
Lands us in a heap of turning leaves,
Turning hearts that ever seek You.

Released from vows,
We pledge again
Our lives to Your keeping,
Our hands to Your work.

Released from vows,
We take up Scrolls
And dancing past the fading moon
We cling to them into *Cheshvan*.

In *Cheshvan*, the tales of wonder and beginnings
Excite the memory of our people;
In *Cheshvan*, the rain and drifting leaves
Exhort us to make ready for leaner times.

You take us into *Cheshvan*:
Listening to our hearts.

You take us into *Cheshvan*,
Singing our hearts to the Eternal.

# ONE HUNDRED TWO
*14 Cheshvan 5755*

Abram, Sarai, transformed, renamed;
How did they know Who called?
To leave loved familiar, set out on a pledge.
How could their new faith hold?

Why Abraham, why Sarah?
Hearing Your promise,
Beginning a journey to You
That held against enemies.

How will I know Your call?
How will I translate Your summons?
Setting out from illness to health
On this pledge of modern miracles?

Journey me toward You, my Healing God,
Walking my path of hope.
Lighten my step with Sarah's laughter,
With Abraham's faith in Your might.

# ONE HUNDRED THREE
*At The Kallah*
*For P.S.K.*

Here within Covenant's circle,
Our feet measure new dance steps
To Torah's living melodies,
Swaying, bowing to praise Your Name.

Here within Covenant's circle,
We struggle to reconcile this world
With Your world, our deeds
With the ways of our ancestors.

Here, dancing past, Abraham and Sarah,
Moving toward an unknown Land;
Here, moving slowly, the despair of generations,
The torn remnant returning.

Here we are, Eternal One:
Not on the circle's edge, not in its middle
But moving, dancing, accommodating our steps
To keep Your tempo in a changing world.

Here are You, Eternal One:
Watching our dance, tapping in time
To the cosmic melody as Your people
Find new ways to honor You.

Here within Covenant's circle,
Let us dance sacred rhythms,
Turning wisely, stepping lovingly,
As we sanctify Your Name.

# ONE HUNDRED FOUR
*Rosh Chodesh Kislev*

Abruptly, the darkness descends upon us.
Your hand tilts the earth toward colder times
We scurry to close the day's moments
As sun rays vanish before we are ready.

All the months we rush about scrambling,
Trying to pack more in each day's basket,
Fleeing the darkness
By filling the days with lightning steps.

Then, abruptly, *Kislev*
When our Mothers labored in tents
To birth the Nation Israel.
In their pangs they called upon Your Name.

Women's voices calling:
Lean upon the Eternal
In the failing light, in pain and darkness.

Gather in new tents.
Move through darkness to the fire-lit places
To praise Your Name together.

# ONE HUNDRED FIVE
*Chanukah*
*For R.M.P.*

Colder, darker, damp in the bones:
It is the last light of *Kislev*,
The season of miracles,
When You worked wonders.

I stalk the midnight house,
Alone awake in darkness,
And find my miracle:
Sweet love sleeping as I roam.

Here is my miracle, Wonder-Maker:
Not the oil that burned too long,
But this lasting flame of faithfulness
That does not extinguish.

Here is my wonder, Miracle-Maker:
That Your words overwhelm me,
Trouble me, consume me with new wonders,
Even as they struggle for animation.

It is the season of wonders,
When Your miracles become comfortable;
The daily gracefulness of life
Belies earthbound discomforts.

It is the season of miracles,
When the wonders that sustain me
Become threads of brilliance, flames
Soaring upwards to honor You.

# ONE HUNDRED SIX
*In Sanibel*

At this latitude, changeling winter warmth,
Here between the ocean-sky,
I consider Your heavens
And Your sweet-singer of praises.

I consider Your heavens, dark night,
Clear with rising moon sliver;
I consider Your heavens and startled,
Know *Dovid ha-Melech* saw just these stars.

This brief moment, this clarity of stars
Points the way to ancient holiness,
The unchanging connection, slender, potent,
That You send us through their constancy.

I consider Your heavens.
You are mindful of me.
I consider Your heavens
With my mind full of You.

# ONE HUNDRED SEVEN
*Erev Rosh Chodesh Adar I*

You lull me with winter sun and central heating;
I lull myself with excuses:
This comfortable nest compounded of
    my infirmity,
My requirements, my cautions against icy
    winds.

You hear me, O Eternal, wherever I call You.
You hear me in my dressing gown
As easily as my dress-up clothes,
And I soothe myself with hot tea and
    on-line Torah.

Winter sun that warms my face
Rekindles my longing for community:
More than visitors and correspondents,
Phone callers and messengers.

Help me to evaluate my strength, O Eternal,
Weighing the risks of reality with the yearning
Of these weeks of isolation,
Breathing the same air I have breathed before.

Help me, O Eternal, to fortify my courage
With Your energy and Your kind regard
As I bundle my weakness in overcoats
And wrap a scarf of caution against winter winds.

# ONE HUNDRED EIGHT
*Rosh Chodesh Adar I*

Where is Esther secluded in this false *Adar*?
Your moon cycles twice before we meet her,
As we take this stagger step
That *Pesach* arrives burgeoning.

Would You have us tread the living waters,
Moving in place while the season turns?
Or shall we kick off in a new direction,
Stroking forward through filtered winter light?

Perhaps like Esther, we shall spend the days
In handwork and sewing, in finely drawn letters
That line out the sweet morsels of Torah
To hang them before our eyes.

Or use the time to restack memories,
Consolidating new vocabularies to fashion praises,
To move the boxes of monotony and clear a space
To assemble our sacred obligations.

We shall sing quietly as we await the moon's path,
Chanting together the well-loved words;
We will ready our feet to be happy in the next
cycle,
Incorporating this interlude to Your honor.

# ONE HUNDRED NINE

*14 Adar I*
**After Heart Studies**

Caught, incarcerated,
Pressure-dressed and peering through bars,
*Adar's* extra moon catches me, exposes me,
Draws me back to You.

Here, O Eternal Healer, the red ribbon of my faith
Is tested, tied to technologies' magic.
Here, O Eternal Healer, I place my trust
In the keen minds of Your creations.

And the purposeless moon, the place-holding
     moon,
Is called to my revelation:
To draw me on toward healing,
To draw me on.

# ONE HUNDRED TEN

*A Women's Song*
*For B.L.M.*

Help me to name myself, Name Maker,
Recapturing the purity of soul
Your Finger placed within me
As I sighed my first earth breath.

Then I was daughter, child, mother-image;
Line-continuer in a way unknown to males.
The blood of bone of Your chosen:
Mine to be, mine to offer.

Now daughter to a different generation,
My name wobbles and crashes in mourning.
Call my name as I struggle to be daughter,
Coping with changes:
Mother caught, me caught, probing for solidity.

Call my name through lives and sorrows:
Friends and husbands and children,
Twirling and swerving, parting, joining.
Call me through rejections and agonies,
When my hands are not enough and my
    offerings wither.

Redefine me as the colors shift and change,
As I grow older, as my needs are muted or
   exposed.
Find the new name I answer when challenged,
A name that is respected and obeyed;
Whisper the pet name that smiles at me from
   memory.

Name me as I name myself, but more gently.
Unfold the arms held tight across my breasts
And pour again Your affection upon my heart.
Strengthen me with memory of Your finger touch,
Renaming this soul You have placed with love.

# ONE HUNDRED ELEVEN

*A Song for First Childbirth*
*For E.G.S.*

In the midst of my sorting and stacking,
In the midst of my clearing and putting,
You call me with insistent flutters.
You call me to begin.

Your hand points the right path;
You guide me to the starting place.

In the lightness of the early journey,
I praise You for readiness.
I praise You for body strength.
I praise You for spirit's song.

Your hand gestures the smooth beginning;
You mark the easy trail upward.

I change and expand through this holy journey,
Given to my guarding,
Given to my being as I climb with effort,
Secure in Your love for me.

Your hand holds aside the undergrowth;
You clear the path before me.

I change again and look behind me,
Seeking the trail I have paced,
Wishing for retreat and solace;
Yet You comfort me and draw me on.

Your hand moves me forward;
You renew my strength.

Then above me, Your hand hovers, blesses;
A Finger of radiance presses this new being.
Sweet healthy cries
In counterpoint to my own thanksgiving song.

Your Loving hand guards me in all my journeys;
You move me safely to new beginnings.

# ONE HUNDRED TWELVE
*Shabbat Afternoon in Sivan*
*For H.J.L.*

In this sun and shadow of *Shabbat* reverie,
Sitting amidst my papers and my teacup,
In this sweet place of midsummer greens,
I hear Your murmur.

You murmur: "Still."
You whisper: "Yes."
Gently, patiently, You soothe me,
Bringing *Shabbat* sighs to free my soul.

In this warmth of *Shabbat* afternoon,
Setting aside worries for this timeless time,
Clearing and coaxing my soul,
I listen to Your quiet call.

I fold my papers and sip my tea.
Leaning back, I breathe deeply:
No inventories, no questions, no plans.
Just this perfect rest to honor You.

Not sleep, but more than sleep;
Not study, but more than study.
I sit gently and give thanks
As I murmur "Yes."

# ONE HUNDRED THIRTEEN
*For Leaving*

You divide our attentions, Courage Builder,
Growing callouses around our affections
So the fingers playing out these tunes of loss
Are toughened against the leaving.

You wander with us through aisles of distractions,
Holding our lists, binding up our abrasions
With reminders of practicalities, touches
That lend reality to our intention.

You divide our attentions, Courage Builder
With Your call to focus, to function,
To make new arrangements for changed days
Even as we shrink from imagining.

You are there for us, Holy One,
Bearing the unadorned truth of love
That holds and holds and then lets go,
Honoring Your design.

# ONE HUNDRED FOURTEEN
*Infertility*

To all the natural world,
The benediction of Your first *mitzvah*,
The multiplicity of plants and souls
Filling the land, controlling.

To all the natural world,
The tan cheeked, rosy cheeked darlings
Whose bodies dive and rise,
Doves and roses in the sacred dance.

To all the natural world,
I who have praised You, prayed You,
Honored and learned You,
Poring over texts, pouring out my heart.

To all the natural world
Of discoveries and interventions,
Orchestrated with *tehillim* by rainy windows
And weeping in the night.

To this unnaturalness of denial,
Emptiness, unenfoldedness, uncontrolled.
Cycles of belief and dismay, gloom, distrust.
The stilled expectations of hearts' faith.

To all this, O Eternal One,
To all this I search for my release,
My place in circled arms, my arms circling,
My grief spent.

# ONE HUNDRED FIFTEEN
*Erev Rosh Hashanah*

Shocked as summer's waited days
Change in an instant to autumn winds,
I shake myself, rushing, running
To catch hold of the season's turning.

Where have I been?
What have I hurried after
That pressed against *Yamim Noraim*
I am not ready.

Calm me as I turn to You, Beloved One.
Accept my jumbled thoughts and order them,
Quiet them, untangle these words
That seek to honor and praise You.

While I scramble over immediacies,
Open the door of my life.
Beloved One, unlatch my heart
And clear the path to You.

Looking ahead, I embrace the preparations
That have brought me to this day:
New doors in existing frames,
Changes to honor You, turning, turning.

# ONE HUNDRED SIXTEEN

*For Changes*
*Outside the Student Union*

Sometimes You ask me to stand still.
And trembling, gasping for a calm center,
I gather in the flying limbs of my frenzy,
Even as I thrash against this amber capture.

Sometimes You ask me to hold tight.
With faint belief in my own courage,
I wrap my limbs in fixed contractures
Even as I turn my head to hide the weeping.

Sometimes You ask me to move on.
Against my pleading, my shout for clock's
    unturning,
You birth me again and again,
Your guiding hand forever steady.

Sometimes You ask me to let go.
Slowly, persistently, I relax my option,
And discover a spectrum of choices
Contained in Your next chapter.

# ONE HUNDRED SEVENTEEN
*Autumn Wondering*
*For E.L.L.*


In colder winds, swirling, gusting
Leaves of muted hues,
In colder winds,
I call You, O Eternal.

Strengthen my back, as raking into piles
I separate and contemplate
These days and changes,
Crackling and clinging against my heart.

Strengthen my arms as pulling and pulling
I drag this heaped tarpaulin of my dilemmas
To pile high and light with hope's spark,
Burning away the turmoil of these days.

Not the pause before winter's sleep
But a beginning; even as the dormant roots
Take up nourishment
So shall my resolve be nourished by the Eternal.

There, a patch of red and gold still clinging
Guards against selflessness:
Your gift to me as I straighten from raking,
As I push the glowing embers together.

# ONE HUNDRED EIGHTEEN
*For B.L.*

Blessing You I bless myself:
I hold the spark of me before Your eyes
And tremble as I see my reflection,
Holy One to holy one.

Blessing You I bless myself,
For I bless remembering and placing,
Separating, discerning, arranging
Spaces of holiness, moments of benediction.

Blessing You I bless myself,
Triggering ancient words, gestures,
Motions that twine me to before,
To befores without number.

Blessing You I bless myself
As ancient words transform,
Comfortable in this time,
Singing songs for days to come.

Blessing You I bless myself
With knowledge, with goodness and care:
Sacred words for everyday;
Every day for sacredness.

# ONE HUNDRED NINETEEN
*To the Memory of Yitzhak Rabin*

Someday
I will be comforted, Holy One;
I will shudder to silence, wiping tears.
I will gaze into unfocused distance;
I will return to Your Arms.

Someday
I will be comforted, Holy One
With assurance of a steady world,
With dawn's returning,
With the dying of bitter winds.

Someday
I will be comforted, Holy One.
I will turn away horrors;  lighting paths
For the peaceful days to come,
I will return to Your Arms.

# ONE HUNDRED TWENTY
*AIDS*

To survive the high noon of diagnosis,
We found optimistic eyeshades, Holy One,
Blinders of hope for years to come,
Setting our love fast with Your love.

To survive illness' overcast glare,
We pulled out woven hats, Holy One,
Our community of treatments and duties,
A dailyness of life as it was.

To survive the wornaway of days, the nights,
We wrapped ourselves in hooded robes,
Waking in dark hours, Holy One,
Praying near dawn for healing, dreamless sleep.

To survive these ending days,
You draw taut the sheet of courage, Holy One,
Binding us up in spent anger transformed,
In enduring love.

To survive alone,
You draw me to You, Holy One,
Remembering joys of unshaded brightness,
Hatless, uncovered, unscathed.

# ONE HUNDRED TWENTY-ONE
*Midlife Changes*
*For P.S.*


Removing my glasses, I rub my eyes
As softly, Wings settle, just past focus.
And I croon, ever so softly, the hymn
Of my soul's yearning.

These many years of striving, my soul
A clear bell tone
Resounding inside me.  You heard
And I sang back Your echo tone.

You heard as I filled the silences,
Needing to sing more;
Honored, hearing new songs,
Wings fly onward, upward.

I turn and follow the glorious flight
As Shadow spreads over me,
Inviting, sheltering, blessing;
Encouraged, my resolve strengthens.

# ONE HUNDRED TWENTY-TWO

*A Parent's Prayer*
*For S.A.*

I am trying, Life-Arranger, I am trying
To live with uncertainties.
I am trying to yield control,
To listen for the calm beneath.

My task nearly done, I am trying to trust
My nurturing and modeling
Have grown a complete person
Ready to enter the next territory.

All my caring words, instructions
Repeated and reworded are no armor.
Only faith in Your kindness
Will secure each tomorrow.

Letting go my protecting hug,
Releasing my shielding body,
I relax. And then I feel You.
You alone must be the Shield about us.

Only to be whole and to be happy.
Only to be well-loved and productive.
Giving and friendly, untroubled by terrors.
Parents' sighs rise to You.

# ONE HUNDRED TWENTY-THREE
*Plans For the Long-Term*

We dream You, Holy One.
Creating our vision of tomorrow,
We coax sacredness into our lives,
Sharing it abroad to warm the world.

We dream, Holy One, of *pintel Yids*,
Sparks of our souls
Gathering, securing our community
For the times to become.

Holy One, dreaming us sound and whole,
You wake us and place our hands
Together to these tasks,
Together to Your glory, blessing, blessing.

# ONE HUNDRED TWENTY-FOUR
*Tu B'Shevat*

Move me, Source of Strength
From bone frost, tear freeze,
And let my heart gaze at the Golden City,
Jeweled in green trees.

Lift me from here-now.
Let me watch the children come
With plastic buckets, trowels and spades
To plant the nourishing trees.

Nourish my heart, Mind Warmer,
Nourish my mind's eye with this fertile
    redemption.
Let me watch these tender stems of tomorrow's
    strength
As young ones hold them aloft and bless You.

Nourish me with the planting.
Warm me as I begin my own planting,
Burrowing in unsteady ground
To bless Your future plans.

# FROM THE HOSPITAL:

# TEN SONGS FOR HEALING

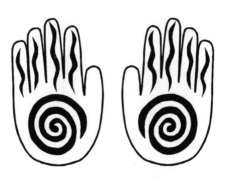

# ONE HUNDRED TWENTY-FIVE

*In the Surgical Waiting Room*
*For B.G.*

Giving my worries over to the waiting,
I step into this apartment of now
You build for me,
A resting place for just these times.

You construct it of hope and memories,
Of great heaving sobs and noisy laughter
That we have collected in equal parts
And stored away to pay this mortgage.

It is a perfect place to just exist,
To read the same sentence again and again,
To start at telephones' jangle,
To lean against Your loving arm.

In this room You guide me, Blessed Healer,
You fortify my strength for this waiting;
In this room You calm me to courage
For the weighted days and nights to come.

# ONE HUNDRED TWENTY-SIX

*A Prayer Before Surgery*
*For S.L.N.*

Stand near, Blessed Healer!
With precision of Divine creation,
Bind and bless,
Seal and straighten,
Heal and make whole.

Stand near, Blessed Healer!
Stand near guiding precise hands
To do Your mending,
Revising life for Your sake.

# ONE HUNDRED TWENTY-SEVEN
*Intensive Care Unit*

Hooked, Holy One, linked and lined,
To openings divine and necessary;
Hooked, Divine Healer, to computer pads,
    data recorders,
Divining and refining every breath and beat.

Hooked to kind friends arriving,
Greeting *Shabbat* with electric bulbs,
Their voices joining as I weep.
Linked to lines, to them, to You.

Hooked, as choking, terrified,
Calm nurse hands move efficiently,
Setting aright, clearing, relieving,
Aligning me toward recovery.

I am hooked, Divine One.
I am hooked to this medicine and this mystery:
The human hands in Your stead,
Guarding and rehearsing my complete healing.

# ONE HUNDRED TWENTY-EIGHT
*Intensive Care Unit*

My heart calls You, Holy One,
My heart bottom, bone marrow,
Flesh of soul of being,
Calls You to my questioning.

My heart calls in the suddenness
Of my distress, and the mute days
When I praise forgetting
And compliance, choice surrendered.

My heart calls You in the wakeful times,
Surfacing, succumbing.  You are there,
Sustaining my momentary consciousness,
Reminding me to praise You in this place.

Ancient words remind me:
I clutch them tightly, syllable and tone.
You hover in their echo, Holy One,
Supporting my courage and my hope.

# ONE HUNDRED TWENTY-NINE
*For the Healers*

You alone, Holy One, You alone.
But sometimes, in the blessed space
Of concert and consideration
We follow Your path toward healing,
Creating stillness in Your Name.

You alone, Holy One, can claim our striving,
Our duties as wholeness descends
In its myriad destinations and definitions,
Our efforts grown to realities.

You alone, Holy One, You alone
Hover in these holied occupations
As our hands move to comfort,
As our hearts embrace this calling.

# ONE HUNDRED THIRTY
*Recovering*

Gasping beneath this waterfall of illness,
Frozen limbs straining,
Lungs pushing against the crash,
Heart crying out with rapid beats.

Gasping, Sacred Healer, frantic
To whisper Your name,
To grasp blessing and power
And raise it above me in shelter.

Torrents overwhelm me,
Drown me in foaming water.
My hand moves, reaching, rising
To protect my face.

Turn to me, Holy One!
Turn back the blasting water,
The pain and sadness,
The shuddering of chances lost.

Turn to me, Sacred Healer!
Multiply my tiny motions
To bring my passage
To dry land.

# ONE HUNDRED THIRTY-ONE
*Going Home*

Strengthen me, Holy One, on my walk
   from illness.
Even as You gave courage
As the children fled from Egypt,
Open the sea to my steps.

Like a Hebrew slave,
I have sojourned in pain;
Under whips of illness and despair,
I have shed my tears of bitterness.

Show me again the path of freedom,
Speeding toward a Promised Land
Of wholeness and health,
Creating my completeness for Your sake.

Bring me up through recovery,
Through remedies and therapies,
To an altered yet acceptable life,
Again rejoicing in the commonplace.

Then will my songs fill this recovered shore,
Where my mind will dance for joy
At my deliverance,
Singing Your praises, Holy One, singing
   new songs.

# ONE HUNDRED THIRTY-TWO

*One Year Later*
*For M.L.*

In that instant, Holy One,
Goading me to choose life,
Hovering, guiding skilled hands
As I hovered, questioning my choice.

In these instances, day by day,
Goading me from terror and doom,
You hover by my right hand,
You steady my left hand.

This is a day for remembrance.
This is the day, where slowly facing
The changes and hurts, I reach out
To replace brokenness with Your touch.

These are the years for remembrance,
Holding memories as guideposts
To future uncertainties,
Held firm with love and faithfulness.

Gather the choices and days;
Gather new routines and restlessness
To transform this enormity
With courage of Your care.

# ONE HUNDRED THIRTY-THREE

*Hospice*
*For A.S., z"l*

Ease me, Holy One.
Soften these rigid arms
That held pain away,
Unwilling it, refusing.

Ease me away from straight arm lifting
Weights of illness and prognosis,
What might have been
And what is.

Holy One, ease my fright of mind drifting
Toward tomorrow and tomorrow.
Ease me to single days: focused, kind;
Ease me to quiet nights: dreamless, calm.

Ease me, Holy One, with memories;
So will I be embraced.
Ease me to Your arms from loving arms:
From hugs to Hug.

# ONE HUNDRED THIRTY-FOUR
*Hospice*

Holding You clearly within my heart,
I pause in my courage;
In that breath space,
You hear my bewilderment.

Holding within my heart Your closeness,
I send small flickers of anger
That devour this utter senselessness,
And then extinguish.

Holding You clearly within my heart,
I loose the bravery, the small talk
And allow my evolution
To reflect Your steadfastness.

Holding You in my very being,
The still place, the me of me,
I release the misery, the hopes lost
And know You gather me in.

Hold me in Your heart, Holy One
As I call upon You in these final days.
Listen as I hold You, Holy One,
My heart transforming, Your dwelling place.

# ONE HUNDRED THIRTY-FIVE

*B'nai Mitzvah Bogrim*
*For P.R.C.*

Timid no more, Holy One:
O all my soul, singing to You!

The words of ancient days,
Honey in my mouth, in my heart;
Even in mature season, I am called.

To this formal declaration,
On sacred space, an anointed time,
Raise my voice to the heavens, Holy One!
All words to Your honor:
Hallelujah!

# ONE HUNDRED THIRTY-SIX
*For Serenity*

As the children grumbled for manna,
So do I mutter to You, my Counselor,
Picking over these pieces of sustenance,
Inspecting them for defects.

And I grumble in my indecision,
My careening attention that worries me.
It pulls the center from my focus,
You call and I am not here.

By day I rustle my lists and memos,
Clouds and piles of tasks and intentions;
Each week finds me further breathless
For completion and healing.

Too much to quantify, verify.
My days stumble out of rhythm,
Left searching for Your holy sound:
My heartbeat, my stillness.

# ONE HUNDRED THIRTY-SEVEN

*A Song For Memory and Honor*
*Sanctuary Rededication*

Surround us, Holy One, with sacred space.
Wrap mature trunks in newer growth,
Sturdy stems blooming in older shade,
Foreshadow of those to come.

Swirl around us a space of holiness,
Of community and truth, of justice and *simcha*,
Winding back to Sinai, rolling forward to
    eternity:
A gathering place, a home-from-home.

Then we shall praise You for courage and vision,
For tasks in partnership with heaven's decree;
All voices gathering, rising to You, Holy One,
Renaming and reclaiming, rejoicing.

# ONE HUNDRED THIRTY-EIGHT
*Uncertainty*

Unspooling duality tangles me
Again and again, my heel catching
In the hem of life's garment,
Stretched long with falling tears.

I seek You in the after glimmer,
After this day's rain of terrible scenes,
New unfolding schemes, new secrets.
You come to calm me, Holy One, with cool light.

You are there with savory goals,
Laid out like a picnic on new grass
To spark an appetite grown weary and becalmed,
Negligent of soul's refreshment.

I think, Holy One, You do not tease
With these delicacies, but rather spread them
For my ease, giving me breathing space
For another day's maneuvers.

# ONE HUNDRED THIRTY-NINE
*Kol Nidre*

Ruler of the Universe!
At our season of renewal,
We are turning, bending,
Viewing front and back.

Ruler of the Universe!
At our season of revival,
We are uncovering, revealing,
Sweeping out.

Ruler of blessing,
We lean upon the Gate,
Testing the hinges,
Rubbing sharp edges.

Ruler of mercy,
We test our souls,
Rubbing fresh cloth over sorrow,
Binding away disappointment.

Called, called to the Gate,
We jostle, then quiet,
As memory and hope
Soothe us.

Standing, striving,
We empty our hearts' longing
Before You, Holy One,
Source of life.

# ONE HUNDRED FORTY
*Thanksgiving Day*

How easy to praise You, Beloved One,
For abundance, for cups brim filled;
How can we not delight in Your majesty,
Your endless blessings to us.

How simple our thanks, Beloved One,
For laden tables, for gathered families,
Shoulders touching in the intimacy of the meal
You have spread before us.

Teach us to thank and bless Your name,
When cups are empty and thirst is great;
Put our hands together to replenish,
Finding blessing in tiny sips.

Beloved One, to thank and bless You,
We find hope in uncertainty
And triumph in shaky steps.
We recreate abundance for Your sake.

# ONE HUNDRED FORTY-ONE
*Chanukah*

*Nes gadol haya sham.*
Holy One, Your miracle of light
Vanquished the darkness of defilement,
Embracing us in holiness.

*Nissim gedolim hayu po.*
Holy One, Your daily miracles
Wait for us, sorting through darkness
To kindle new lights of holiness.

Not eight day lasting oil
But everlasting loyalty and devotion,
Standing as Maccabees against modern blows,
Night terrors of a changing world.

Hold out the single cruse, Holy One,
As we turn our hearts to flame in wonder;
Multiply our ingenuity to see miracles
In this constancy of Your care.

# ONE HUNDRED FORTY-TWO
*A Prayer for Healing*

Strengthen me, Holy One, on my journey through
    illness;
Steady my steps on this difficult path.
Bring me through signposts of remedies
    and therapies,
Secure in Your guidance as I face these changes.

You are my Strength and my Hope,
The Author of my healing.
You are my Promise and my Courage,
Guiding my helpers as I move toward healing.

Guard the encouragement of simple improvements,
Every day praising Your loving concern.
Make me Your partner, Divine Physician,
Restoring me for Your Name's sake.

# ONE HUNDRED FORTY-THREE
*Last Days*

Guide me, Holy One, on this final journey,
Your hand pointing the way,
Your loving eye upon my face
As I seek my new dwelling.

Surround me with Your kindness,
Embrace me with tranquility;
Soothe my fears with the surety of Your care,
Even as I release my tears to Your custody.

Then shall I find Your eternal gift of peace,
Laid out for my notice and my strength.
Linger near, Holy One, through these trials,
Easing my way as I fly to Your keeping.

# ONE HUNDRED FORTY-FOUR

*For the Survivors*

You sound the closing bell, Holy One,
Ringing through time to reshape this future,
Life changing, shattering,
Dreams and hopes revised in an instant.

Unleash the tears and anger
As I offer them to You,
As You take them for healings' sake,
Someday transforming to peace and calm.

Untie me from old bitterness,
From thoughts of should-have-been
As I find strength in Your unchanging concern,
And take succor from the constancy of Your love.

# ONE HUNDRED FORTY-FIVE
*A Song of Healing*
*For S.B.*

Soothe away my fears, Holy One;
Order these difficult days.
Praising You, I reach for healing,
Holding close Your constancy.
In between each today and tomorrow,
Arrange my move toward wholeness.

Bring Your strength to my need!
A mending and a healing,
True and straight.

Every day stronger, I bless You:
Small steps to complete healing.
Trusting You, I accommodate these changes,
Helped by skilled hands,
Embraced by love and concern,
Resting in Your care.

# ONE HUNDRED FORTY-SIX
*Daily Questions*

I am frightened, Holy One,
Of uncertainties.  The questions,
Speculations, unknown futures,
Riddles without answers.

Todays follow in their narrowed path,
New duties, treatments, routines,
All concocted to stabilize.
Yet I distrust their efficiency.

Sliding, slipping, gasping,
Limbs stiff, I hesitate.
No easy climbs, no careless tasks.
Help me to consolidate.

You alone unlock my puzzle,
Lending strength to attempt each day.
Still my fright with words that praise You,
Slow my breath with sustaining Care.

# ONE HUNDRED FORTY-SEVEN

*Contemplating Death*

When I die
I move into Your space, Holy One;
Light and substance
Blend into Your perfect *shalom*.

And my dear ones
Speak my name with Your Name,
Remembering and reflecting
As their tears turn to jewels.

# ONE HUNDRED FORTY-EIGHT
*Shacharit*

With daily repetition of Your blessings,
I slip into the cadences of holiness;
The slowly sounding out of ancient words
Eases into surety and confidence.

You call me, Holy One, to praise You,
And I praise these others' words
To form my offerings and blessings,
Organized, unvaried, ordered in my mouth.

As words relinquish strangeness,
I see the spaces between, the pauses
That offer place for my private yearnings,
My intimate conversation with You.

I praise You, Holy One.
I have learned the words to sing my awakening;
Each morning I praise my soul's return,
Melody for rising, my precious knowledge.

I bless You, Holy One,
As structured sequences empower,
Defining and refining
My steps to You.

# ONE HUNDRED FORTY-NINE

*A Song for Honor*
*For H.J.L.*

As Miriam spoke in clear words for her brother,
Holy One, You guide me to light up Your ways.
Reveal simple gifts that await exploration;
Articulate hope for all of my days.

Open my hand to gather Your goodness,
Sharing it out with unhurried rite.
Gather my strength to notice Your wonder
Hiding in shadows, bursting toward light.

Singing in voices that echo our mothers,
Sarah is laughing but Hannah's in pain;
So will I share all the richness before me,
Blessing my being and blessing Your Name.

# ONE HUNDRED FIFTY

*An Anniversary Song*
*For D.C.K. and J.K.*

You tuned our early melodies, Sweet Singer,
Merging tentative chords,
Resounding with growing love,
To form our early compositions.

You walked with us through ancient streets,
As hand in hand in Hand
We found truth kernels and mislaid dreams
To flavor our affections.

O Beloved One, You bestow joy
And fulfillment with future inheritance,
Children to sustain our hopes
And restate our love.

O Beloved Singer, You clarify the score
Of our life's unrolling stories,
As, bound tightly to Your duties,
Our union sings Your praise.

# ONE HUNDRED FIFTY-ONE
*Erev Rosh Hashanah*

We crowd before the moment of Your Gate's
   release,
Gathering in the holiness of our multitude,
Beginning in this moment of beginning
Our repeated journey to Your heart's place.

Year Renewer, You bless our numbers,
Counting souls found once more
As we enter the sacred Gate,
To name ourselves before Your Presence.

You number every one, every two and more
   together,
Grouping and rehearsing the human dances;
You bless us, every one, in uniqueness and
   sameness,
As we shift and change our places, shimmering
   in light.

We are Your hallowed remnant, Your holy people;
Help us to fulfill our legacy.
Bring to this beginning continued deeds of
   goodness,
New year of holy choices, new year of sacred
   trusts.

# ONE HUNDRED FIFTY-TWO
*Shabbat Shuvah*

Turn me, turn me, return me to You;
Turn me, heal me with grace of *shalom*.
Turn me, my Maker, return me, my Friend,
Return me to *chesed*, to faith, back to Home.

Turn me, turn me, I will return
To build foundations of honor and blessing.
Return me to duty, to love, to repair,
To the work of my hands for Your glory.

Turn me, turn me, return me to You,
Watching creation renewed for my sake.
Turn me, heal me, transform hesitations
To form a new covenant, a holy embrace.

# ONE HUNDRED FIFTY-THREE
*Kol Nidre*

We gather to anticipate, closing Gate, sealing Gate,
Crowding in passing time, opening hearts to You.
Finding in these ending moments, new beginnings
Of faith in our chances for renewal.

Turn us to You, Year Redeemer,
Bless our turning toward humility, humanity,
Tasks that bind us to Your world's repair,
Our souls' repair in this world, in the world
    to come.

Turn us to each other in Your sacred planning,
Conveying Your design in holy choices;
Turned to You with deeds of goodness,
Turned to You in trust and faithfulness.

Seal the Gate for Your holy people,
Seal it with righteousness and truth.
Bring to this Decision continued strength
    and reason:
Bound to You in blessing, bound to You in hope.

# ONE HUNDRED FIFTY-FOUR
*After the Marketplace Bombing*
*For G.S.*


Gather my scattered thoughts, Holy One,
Open my tight held fist.
Loosen my tension, leaning on You,
Dreams calming, days again bright
As I wake to behold the Land's splendor.

Shutter my fears with sweet recall,
Heal wounds of witnessed terrors.
Invent me again for Your blessing:
Renewal and strength, comfort and peace
As I rise to affirm Your glory.

# ONE HUNDRED FIFTY-FIVE

*A Song of Welcome for a Daughter*

Embrace this new daughter with blessing,
   Holy One;
Draw her near to You with learning and faith.
May her life be filled with delight,
Nurtured in wholeness, her family's embrace.

Alert her to all Your world's beauty,
Renewed before her eyes, flowering.
Inspire her with tales of her ancestors,
Enriched by her own good deeds.
Name her with strength and goodness,
A life for Your honor and praise.

# ONE HUNDRED FIFTY-SIX
*A Song of Welcome for a Son*

Draw Your arms around this new son, Holy One,
Let Your blessings be abundant.
May his days be filled with learning,
With wonders and challenges, laughter and delight.

Anchor his life with family and friends,
Kindness his portion and gift;
Send him Your strength to grow and mature,
Keeping close to his strong heritage.
Embrace him with wholeness, with peace,
Ever praising Your name.

# ONE HUNDRED FIFTY-SEVEN
*For Teachers*

Gather these newest sons and daughters,
Open their curiosity and wonder
To find their dawning love for You,
Nurtured by teacher's care.

As You bless them, You bless us, Holy One,
For You validate the future of Your people;
As they find You we find ourselves
Holding their hands through Your people's history.

The earliest *Talmud Torah*, the first steps,
Are strengthened by guidance and devotion,
Made sweet by tenderness and attention,
By hugs and stories and song.

# ONE HUNDRED FIFTY-EIGHT

*A Wedding Song*
*For J.E.A. and A.I.G.*

Joined this day in Israel's house,
Even as our parents heard seven blessings.
No eyes but each others and Yours, Holy One,
Nodding to the ancient words.
It was written in stars,
Fated, *beshert*, beheld by Your love:
Each and no other,
Right and true, precious, dear.

All Loving One, write joy on our union,
Days and nights of trust and caring;
All Loving One, we honor and praise You,
Miracles linger as memories inspire.

# ONE HUNDRED FIFTY-NINE
*Sabbatical*
*For P.S.K.*

Time apart, time away:
Refresh my soul, Eternal One.
Time of learning, time of prayer,
Calm within, serenity.

Fulfilling Your divine decree,
Time of rest to contemplate
A changing world and work again
For its repair, my hand in Yours.

Sacred space in varied clime,
Home transformed, discovery.
Let me find restoring peace,
Your wholeness as my portion.

# ONE HUNDRED SIXTY
*A Song of Praise*

Hallelujah!
I will praise You with all my soul,
My very being, my inside of me,
The core of all that You make holy.

Hallelujah!
I will sing You the spirit's song
Poured into me by Your hand,
Tuned by my chances and challenges.

Hallelujah!
I will bless You with common words
Turned to fire by Your listening,
Flames to heaven.

Hallelujah!
I will call You in my longing
For completeness, for shelter
Beneath Your embracing arms.

Hallelujah!
I will turn to You in faithfulness,
Drying my tears
On the surety of Your care.

Hallelujah!
I will praise You with all my soul,
Breath and being, time and future,
Aligned to You in holiness.

# GLOSSARY

# INDEX TO
# THEMES

# GLOSSARY

*Adar.* The twelfth month of the Jewish calendar. In a leap year, a thirteenth month, called *Adar Sheni* ("Second *Adar*") is added.

*Adar 1.* In a year containing thirteen months, the first month of Adar. The holiday of *Purim* always occurs in *Adar 2* or *Adar Sheni.* See above.

*Ani Adonai Rofecha.* "I am God, Your Physician." The word "*Iyar*" forms an anagram of this phrase.

*Ani L'Dodi V'Dodi Li.* "I am My Beloved's and My Beloved is Mine." A Phrase from the "Song of Songs." The word "*Elul*" forms an anagram of this phrase.

*Av.* The fifth month of the Jewish calendar.

*Avinu Malkeinu.* "Our Father, Our King." A litany recited and sung during the Days of Awe, the High Holy Days.

*B'Dikat Chametz.* "Search for Leavened Bread." A symbolic search for the last remains of leaven conducted on the night before *Pesach* (Passover) begins. The eating of leavened food is prohibited during *Pesach.*

*Beshert.* Yiddish. "Fated." Meant to be.

*B'nai Mitzvah Bogrim.* A phrase associated with the contemporary practice of adults celebrating being called to the Torah for the first time.

*Chanukah.* "Dedication; Consecration." The Feast of Lights. *Chanukah* begins on the 25th day of *Kislev* and lasts for eight days. It commemorates the victory of Judah Maccabee and his followers over the forces of the Syrian tyrant Antiochus Epiphanies (165 B.C.E.) and the rededication of the Temple in Jerusalem.

*Chazan.* "Cantor."

*Cheshvan.* The eighth month of the Jewish calendar.

*Chuppah.* The traditional bridal canopy, beneath which the marriage ceremony takes place.

*Dovid ha-Melech.* "King David."

*Elul.* The sixth month of the Jewish calendar.

*Erev Yontiff.* Yiddish, "Before (evening of) the holiday."

*Erev Shabbat.* "Evening of Sabbath." This refers especially to Friday afternoon and early evening.

*Etrog.* (pl.: *Etrogim*). "Citron." One of the four species gathered on *Sukkot*, the fall harvest festival.

*Far Yontiff.* Yiddish, "After the holiday."

*Hallel.* Songs of praise. Traditionally, David's Psalms 113-118 recited on *Rosh Chodesh* and the Festivals.

*Haman.* The vizier in the court of King Ahashuerus who sought the annihilation of the Jewish people because *Mordechai*, Queen Esther's cousin, refused to prostrate himself before him.

*Iyar.* The second month of the Jewish calendar.

*Kibud Av V'Aym.* "Honor Father and Mother."

*Kislev.* The ninth month of the Jewish calendar.

*Kol Nidre.* "All Vows." A declaration of the annulment of all vows with which the evening service of *Yom Kippur* begins.

*Midrashim.* (sing.: *midrash*). "Stories." Usually refers to stories elaborating on stories in the Bible.

*Mishpocheh.* "Family."

*Mitzvot.* (sing.: *mitzvah*). "Commandment." Good deed, religious duty.

*Mordechai.* A Jew who lived in Shushan, the residence of the Persian king Ahashuerus (Xerxes I) who reigned from 486 to 465 B.C.E. He was foster father to his cousin, Esther who was chosen by the king to replace the deposed queen, *Vashti*. *Mordechai* was the only one who refused to bow down to *Haman*, the king's vizier.

*Nes gadol haya sham.* "A great miracle happened there." A phrase associated with the holiday of *Chanukah*, referring to the single cruse of oil that lasted eight days and the miracle of the victory of the Maccabees over the greater Roman troops.

*Nissim gedolim hayu po.* "Great miracles happen here." A variation of the previous phrase.

*Nisan.* The first month of the Jewish calendar.

*Pesach.* "Passover." Spring festival, beginning on the 15th day of *Nisan* and lasting for seven days. It commemorates the Israelite Exodus from Egypt, with the concept of freedom as its main theme. It is called "*Pesach*" or "Passover" because God "passed over" or protected the houses of the children of Israel. *Pesach* is also the paschal lamb that was offered as a sacrifice on the eve of the feast in Temple times.

*Pintel Yids.* Yiddish. Jewish souls; the spark of being a committed Jew.

*Purim.* "Lots." The holiday commemorating the deliverance of the Jews of ancient Persia from *Haman's* plot to kill them, through the efforts of *Mordechai* and Queen Esther. *Purim* ("lots") is so called after the lots cast by *Haman* in order to determine the month in which the slaughter was to take place. The holiday is celebrated on the 14th day of *Adar*. In leap years, it is celebrated during the Second *Adar*.

*Pushke*. Yiddish. "Charity box."

*Rosh Chodesh*. "The New Moon, the New Month." The first day of the month.

*Rosh Hashanah*. "Head of the Year." The Jewish New Year. Celebrated on the first day of *Tishri*. The holiday initiates a period of soul-searching and reflection that culminates on *Yom Kippur*.

*Shabbat*. "Sabbath." The time from Friday sundown until Saturday sundown. The seventh day of the week, an occasion for rest and spiritual refreshment, abstention from the concerns of the workaday world, and participation in home and synagogue religious observances.

*Shabbat Shuvah*. The *Shabbat* between *Rosh Hashanah* and *Yom Kippur*. Its name is derived from the first word of the *Haftarah* read on that Shabbat (Hosea 14:2-10), which begins "*Shuvah Yisrael*" ("Return, O Israel").

*Shacharit*. The morning prayer.

*Shalom*. "Peace." Used as a greeting. Also signifies wholeness, completeness.

*Shamash*. "Servant." The auxiliary candle used to light the eight *Chanukah* candles.

*Shavuot*. "Weeks." A festival celebrated on the 6th day of *Sivan*, seven weeks ("a week of weeks") after Passover. The holiday is also called *Chag Hakatsir* ("The Harvest Festival"), *Chag Habikurim* ("The Festival of First Fruits"), and *Zeman Matan Toratenu* ("The Season of the Giving of the Torah").

*Shevat*. The eleventh month of the Jewish calendar.

*Sh'ma*. "Hear." The first word of the watchword of the Jewish faith: "Hear, O Israel, the Eternal is Our God, the Eternal is One." Recited twice a day, and historically, by martyrs as they met their deaths.

*Shofar*. An animal's horn prepared for use as the ritual horn sounded on *Rosh Hashanah* and *Yom Kippur*.

*Simchat Torah*. "Rejoicing of the Torah." The festival marking the annual completion and recommencing of the Torah-reading cycle.

*Sivan*. The third month of the Jewish calendar.

*Talmud Torah*. "The study of Torah." The *mitzvah* of Jewish study. The term is also applied to the school where one studies Torah and Judaica.

*Tammuz.* The fourth month in the Jewish calendar.

*Tehillim.* Psalms; the Biblical Book of Psalms.

*Teshuvah.* "Return." Repentance, denoting a return to God after sin, or a turning back to God.

*Tevet.* The tenth month of the Jewish calendar.

*Tisha B'Av.* "Ninth of *Av.*" A day of mourning commemorating the destruction of the first and second Temples in Jerusalem as well as other tragic events in Jewish history.

*Tishri.* The seventh month of the Jewish calendar.

*Torah.* The first five books of the Hebrew Bible. Usually referring to the handwritten parchment scroll.

*Tu B'Shevat.* "The fifteenth of *Shevat.*" A minor holiday, designated as the "New Year of the Trees." A time in Israel when trees are planted and when people in the Diaspora send funds to plant trees in Israel.

*Yad.* "Hand." Pointer, usually silver and in the shape of a pointing hand, that the Torah reader uses to follow the words in the scroll. (The surface of the scroll is never touched with the bare hand.)

*Yahrtzeit.* The anniversary of a death.

*Yamim Noraim.* "Days of Awe." The period from the first day of *Rosh Hashanah* until *Yom Kippur* and these two days in particular.

*Yom Hashoah.* "Holocaust Day." The 27th of *Nisan* is set side as a memorial to the victims of the Holocaust.

*Yom Kippur.* "Day of Atonement." A solemn day of fasting and prayer concluding the ten days of penitence that began on *Rosh Hashanah.*

*Z"L.* Abbreviation for *Zichron Livracha.* "Re-membering for a blessing;" "Of blessed memory." Typically added when the name of a deceased person is written or spoken.

Many of the Glossary entries are quoted or adapted from Knobel, Peter S., ed. *Gates of the Seasons: A Guide To The Jewish Year.* New York: Central Conference of American Rabbis, 1983, and are used with permission of the publisher.

# A NOTE ON CALENDARS

The Jewish year follows a different set of rhythms
from the secular year. Each week focuses toward
*Shabbat*, the period of rest and holiness, gladness
and wholeness that lasts from sundown Friday
until three stars appear in the sky on Saturday.

The months follow the lunar cycle; it is important
that *Rosh Hashanah* fall at the New Moon, that
*Sukkot* and *Pesach* begin at the Full Moon. My
songs for *Rosh Chodesh*, the New Moon, try to
reflect the particular flavors of the seasons,
liturgically and temporally.

Judaism recognizes several kinds of new years.
In Torah, *Nisan* is called the first month
(Exodus 12:18), perhaps because it was the time
when the Israelites moved together toward freedom
to became a unified people.

*Tishri* marks the beginning of the new calendar
year; the cycle of the Jewish year begins in *Tishri*.
The preceding month, *Elul*, is preparation for the
ten days of self-examination that begins on *Rosh
Chodesh Tishri*, which is *Rosh Hashanah* and end
on *Yom Kippur*. In this book, both new years, as
well as the "New Year of the Trees," *Tu B'Shevat*,
are referenced. The months are listed in order in
the Index under *Rosh Chodesh*.

# INDEX TO THEMES

## CREATIVITY & SOLUTIONS

## HEALING